"Cristina Pérez Díaz's translation
Watanabe's *Antígona*, as distinct fro
Ralli of the Peruvian theatre group Yuyachkani, to offer a rich interpreta-
tion of this unique theatrical collaboration."

*Helene P. Foley, Claire Tow Professor of Classics,
Barnard College, Columbia University*

"Pérez Díaz's impassioned essays array a dizzying spectrum of political and
cultural referents, while her translation follows Watanabe's lead in constructing a timeless Sophoclean world that foregoes explicit reference to
anything local, in our place and time, or his: the battle against a culture of
oblivion exists everywhere and never ends."

*Esther Allen, Baruch College,
City University of New York*

"Cristina Pérez Díaz's beautiful translation of José Watanabe's *Antígona*
brings this modern classic of Latin American theater to an English audience for the first time. This volume offers a critical introduction to this
poignant play; written in the aftermath of Peru's long civil conflict (1980–
2000), it thematizes the country's process of truth and reconciliation, thus
engaging enduring themes of memory and politics that have characterized
Latin American theater of the past fifty years. Watanabe's play was created
in collaboration with Peru's premiere theater company, Grupo Cultural
Yuyachkani; Cristina Pérez Díaz demonstrates how this version of the classic Antigone story thus engages complex dynamics of adaptation and embodiment. This critical edition of the play is a most welcome addition to
scholarship on Latin American theater, and will be of interest to students
and scholars in the field as well as readers of contemporary drama."

Jill Lane, New York University

ANTÍGONA BY JOSÉ WATANABE

This book brings to English readers, in its entirety for the first time, a translation of José Watanabe's *Antígona*, accompanied by the original Spanish text and critical essays.

The lack of availability in English has resulted in the absence of *Antígona* from important Anglophone studies devoted specifically to the reception of ancient Greek tragedy in the Americas. Pérez Díaz's translation fills this gap. The introduction provides the performative, political, and historical contexts in which the text was written in collaboration with the actress Teresa Ralli, from the Peruvian theatre group Yuyachkani, who also originally performed it. Following the bilingual text, a critical essay provides an analysis of textual aspects of *Antígona* that have been disregarded, situating it in relation to Sophocles' *Antigone* and in conversation with relevant moments of the vast traditions of reception of the Greek tragedy. An appendix briefly surveys some notable productions of the play throughout Latin America.

This comprehensive volume provides an invaluable resource for readers interested in José Watanabe's work, students and scholars working on classical reception and Latin American literature and theatre, as well as theatre practitioners.

Cristina Pérez Díaz translates from Ancient Greek, Latin, and Spanish and is currently a Doctoral Candidate in Classics at Columbia University.

Classics and the Postcolonial

Edited by Rosa Andújar and Justine McConnell, King's College London.

Classics and the Postcolonial publishes monographs, critical editions, and essay collections that explore the invocations and uses of Graeco-Roman antiquity in postcolonial contexts across the globe. Though the emphasis is on the postcolonial, our scope is deliberately broad and includes books which interrogate issues stemming from, and intersecting with, colonialism and imperialism, such as migration, slavery, race, gender, and sexuality. The series brings Classical and Postcolonial Studies into direct dialogue with each other, providing a space for cutting-edge work conducted at the intersection of the two fields.

In addition to scholarly monographs and edited volumes, we warmly welcome proposals for critical editions and anthologies of dramatic and poetic texts. These may be of works originally written in any language, which adapt or engage with Graeco-Roman antiquity in exceptional and varied ways, whether to address sociopolitical realities or to speak to creative concerns.

If you are interested in contributing to the series, please contact the series editors, Rosa Andújar and Justine McConnell (both at King's College London), to discuss your project.

Antígona by José Watanabe
A Bilingual Edition with Critical Essays
Cristina Pérez Díaz

ANTÍGONA BY JOSÉ WATANABE

A Bilingual Edition with Critical Essays

Cristina Pérez Díaz

Routledge
Taylor & Francis Group

LONDON AND NEW YORK

Cover image: Emanuel Torres Pérez

First published 2023
by Routledge
4 Park Square, Milton Park, Abingdon, Oxon OX14 4RN

and by Routledge
605 Third Avenue, New York, NY 10158

Routledge is an imprint of the Taylor & Francis Group, an informa business

British Library Cataloguing-in-Publication Data
A catalogue record for this book is available from the British Library

ISBN: 978-0-367-71338-6 (hbk)
ISBN: 978-0-367-71336-2 (pbk)
ISBN: 978-1-003-15035-0 (ebk)

DOI: 10.4324/9781003150350

Typeset in Bembo
by codeMantra

To my uncle Eli, *in memoriam*

CONTENTS

ACKNOWLEDGMENTS

Many friends read the earliest versions of this translation, and I would have never completed it without their patient comments and corrections. I want to thank especially David Skeist, Noah Davies-Mason, and Aron Shapiro for those patient readings. I do not have enough words to thank my dear friend Jacqui Cornetta, who read and commented on several versions of the translation and improved it considerably. Other friends helped with other things at different times throughout the many years that it took me to write this book, and their affective and intellectual support and inspiration also made this publication possible: Pelé Sánchez Tormes, Laura Torres Rodríguez, Kira Josefsson, and Ezequiel Zaidenwerg.

The Center for the Humanities at the CUNY Graduate Center was kind to help me organize a staged reading of the translation, with friends from the theater company Caborca (David Skeist, Javier Antonio González, and Tania Molina). It was a helpful moment in my process, and I am deeply grateful to everyone involved. I thank David Schur and Margaret Carson, who participated with me in a panel following the staged reading and kindly gave feedback on the translation, encouraging me to publish it. Jean Graham-Jones' reading was also very generous. I'm immensely grateful to Karen Van Dyck at Columbia University for her comments and encouragement as well. The Classics Department at Columbia supported me through the Lodge Fund, and I thank Joseph Howley in particular for securing the help.

I also want to thank *Asymptote Journal*, especially Lee Yew Leong (Editor-in-Chief) and Caridad Tamayo (Drama Editor) for publishing excerpts of the translation in the Spring 2022 issue.

I am enormously indebted to Maya Watanabe and to Micaela Chirif, who were kind to Skype with me when I was just beginning my research on this text and shared valuable information and resources. Teresa Watanabe received me in her home in Lima and showed me the documents in José Watanabe's personal archives. She talked extensively with me about their family and her brother José and warmly introduced me to Ana Gispert, a Professor of Ancient Greek with whom Watanabe consulted while writing *Antígona*. Professor Gispert and her husband received me one lovely afternoon in their apartment in Lima and shared their memories.

I also want to thank Nancy Worman for her support, from the book proposal to the final manuscript. Marcus Folch was also very kind to read a draft of the book proposal. My editors at Routledge, Rosa Andújar and Justine McConnell, have been fundamental interlocutors throughout, for whom I am deeply grateful.

I cannot express my gratitude to Helene Foley enough, who has uninterruptedly supported my work since I first met her as a Professor of Greek in a class at Columbia as a Post-Baccalaureate student in 2012. Professor Foley has seen this project evolve since its early beginnings and without her support, this book would simply not exist.

Finally, I want to thank my parents, Minerva Díaz Adorno and José Miguel Pérez Otero, for their unconditional presence, patience, solidarity, and love.

PREFACE

It is a pleasure to launch *Classics and the Postcolonial* with Cristina Pérez Díaz's edition of José Watanabe's *Antígona*. Making accessible the rich range and variety of postcolonial engagements with Graeco-Roman antiquity across the globe is central to the aims of the series. Pérez Díaz's lucid translation makes this fascinating adaptation of Sophocles' *Antigone* available for the first time to Anglophone audiences, while the bilingual format additionally enables the study of the original text in Spanish.

Given the context in which it was created, *Antígona* has often been read as a commentary on the Peruvian experience of state-sanctioned violence from 1980 to 2000. Pérez Diaz, however, adopts a different approach: she goes beyond historicist readings that risk confining the text to its original context and instead focuses on Watanabe's complex literary aesthetics. With particular attention to key issues of adaptation, affect, and memory, her edition illuminates how Watanabe's text transcends its particular historical and political circumstances.

This broader approach is key when dealing with adaptations of ancient Greek and Roman literature. Similarly, while the emphasis in the *Classics and the Postcolonial* series is on the postcolonial, its scope is deliberately capacious. It includes interrogations of issues stemming from, and intersecting with, colonialism and imperialism, including migration, slavery, race, gender, and sexuality, as well as artistic considerations of adaptation and performance in relation to both antiquity and modernity. As such, we are delighted to inaugurate the series with Pérez Diaz's compelling vision of Watanabe's celebrated play.

Rosa Andújar
Justine McConnell

1
INTRODUCTION

Writing *Antígona*: José Watanabe and Teresa Ralli's collaborative process

The text I am presenting here, *Antígona*, was originally the script for a performance written by José Watanabe in collaboration with actress Teresa Ralli and her director Miguel Rubio, both founding members of the Peruvian experimental and independent theater group Grupo Cultural Yuyachkani. They commissioned *Antígona* as a script for a solo performance by Ralli, based on Sophocles' *Antigone*, but adapted to the specific needs of the actress and connected to their contemporary reality. The constraint that a single actress would perform the entire text had consequences for the form of the script: a series of isolated poems/monologues linked by a narrator. Yet the path went both ways; once Watanabe started writing the poems that would eventually become the final script, the actress' work and performance was in turn affected by the demands and possibilities that the new texts by Watanabe brought with them. As Ralli recounts in her talk *El desmontaje de Antígona* (Disassembling Antígona), she was at first surprised at the prospect of performing an entire "play" in the form of poems: "one day Watanabe came to rehearsal and said, 'But I am a poet! Why don't I write poems?' At first that startled me, because I thought... well, an entire piece of more than an hour in duration saying only poems ..... However, we gave ourselves to the challenge."[1] And so, both in Ralli's original performance of *Antígona* and in Watanabe's written text (published in this

DOI: 10.4324/9781003150350-1

volume), there are imprints of a two-way dialogue between the theater practitioners and the poet, between the stage and the page. In fact, the actress' work precedes the collaboration. In 1998, long before Watanabe joined the creative team, Ralli and Rubio began working on this piece, using a Spanish translation of Sophocles' *Antigone* as a point of departure for their stage research.[2] They worked without a script, following Yuyachkani's own postmodern methodology, in which the actors work with the director to produce stage materials through improvisations with objects and different kinds of textual and visual sources, not privileging the role of the script over other stage elements in the production of meaning, as I discuss below. Their aim, as Ralli recounts in the published essay "Fragments of Memory" and in *El desmontaje de Antígona*, was to use the ancient Greek story to talk about what had been happening in their country over the past two decades. Peru had been suffering a prolonged armed conflict between successive governments and Sendero Luminoso (Shining Path)—a Maoist radicalized political party that in 1980 declared a revolutionary war against the elected government, in the mostly rural and Quechua-speaking highland region of Ayacucho.[3] This conflict, as the *Final Report* by the Commission for Truth and Reconciliation (CVR) would later reveal in 2003, left a toll of 69,280 violently murdered people and/or *desaparecidos*[4] as well as 600,000 displaced peasants, 40,000 orphan children, 20,000 widows, and many other human rights violations, including torture and rape.[5] Furthermore, the effects of the armed conflict in Peruvian society had implications well beyond the number of victims. As Orin Stern writes, the conflict "destroyed political third paths between the poles of violent revolution and a militarized state, and drastically transformed the country" (3).

Ralli was moved to pursue her long-time interest in the story of the Greek heroine at a time when the internal violence was diminishing, after the capture and imprisonment, in 1992, of Shining Path's leader Abimael Guzmán (along with nineteen of twenty-two members of the party's Central Committee). The subsiding of the armed violence, however, had come at a great price. Then-President Alberto Fujimori (1990–2000) used the conflict as an excuse to advance his neoliberal agenda, the militarization of the state, and large-scale schemes of corruption.[6] Fujimori also controlled the narrative of the armed conflict, presenting himself as a savior, numerically misrepresenting the actual number of fatal victims and fostering a culture of oblivion.[7] In spite of the President's efforts, however, in the last years of the 1990s, civic agents began to challenge this narrative and the real dimensions of the decades-long violence began to reach civil society (even though the CVR was not created until 2001). Faced with the stories of victims and the roles that circumstances forced different agents in the civil sphere to take on—especially poor indigenous young women, who overwhelmingly suffered the consequences of the conflict[8]—Ralli and Rubio found themselves called to engage Ralli's long interest in the myth of Antigone ("Fragments" 356). In fact, during the staging process, Ralli interviewed women who had survived the conflict and had organized the Committee of Families of the Disappeared, and her *Antígona* aims to be both a vehicle of their experiences and an homage to their fight and to "their memories inscribed on their bodies" (361–2). Eventually, Yuyachkani would present *Antígona* and other shows concerned with the armed conflict in Ayacucho and other communities harshly affected by the violence, both before and during the public hearings organized by the CVR (361ff).[9]

During the creative process, Ralli and Rubio studied carefully the Sophoclean text. Then, they worked following Yuyachkani's usual approach, building the play not down from a script but up from a process they call "acumulación sensible" (sensorial accumulation)[10]—a practice the company has developed over fifty years of uninterrupted production.[11] This practice ought to be situated against the background of a worldwide change in theater aesthetics that began in the 1960s and 1970s, when practitioners around the world turned against the authority of the written text (along with discourses on the death of the author). In Europe and the United States, this has come to be known as "postdramatic theater."

In the book *Postdramatic Theater*, the German theater scholar Hans-Thies Lehman gave international currency to the term—expanding on prior theorizations by directors such as Richard Schechner—exemplified by movements on European and US American theatrical stages that, after Brecht, experimented with ways of generating meaning in performance that overturned the hierarchical place of the dramatic text and of narrative linearity.[12] Postdramatic practices pay special attention to the semantic capacities of the actors' bodies and the objects on stage and are characterized by strong self-awareness on the part of the actors, who always attempt to go beyond Aristotelian representation or mimesis, often even underscoring the performance's own mechanisms—for example, commenting on their actions or the text they are using or on something that emphasizes the co-present of performers and audience—(*Postdramatic Theater* 36–8).

It is important to emphasize that, while Lehman's case studies are limited to Europe and the United States, the theatrical phenomenon he terms "postdramatic" expands well beyond those borders. Many theater groups in Latin America that began working in the 1960s and 1970s, concurrently with their European and US American peers, developed their own kind of postdramatic aesthetics, also influenced by Brecht and, equally as crucial, by local and indigenous performance, festive, and religious traditions. In fact, some European practitioners who Lehman considers part of the postdramatic turn in theater, like Eugenio Barba and Jerzy Grotowski, are strongly aligned with the postdramatic tradition that developed in Latin America, as they claim belonging to a distinct movement named by Barba himself as the "Third Theatre" (Watson 201). This specifically encompasses theater groups that not only broke with modernist and classical theatrical practices but were also working on the margins of state and private institutions. This Third Theatre developed over a period of four decades in exchanges between European and Latin American theater groups that shared an ethos of anti-institutional and anti-capitalist practices.[13] As Ian Watson puts it: "The Third Theatre, a concept first suggested by Eugenio Barba in 1976, is an idea that was born in Europe but one that has been subsequently shaped by Latin America" (201). Yuyachkani have been essential contributors to the development of this movement since they participated in the "Third Encounter of Third Theatre,"[14] organized by Peruvian director Mario Delgado in Ayacucho, Peru in May of 1978, with the support of Eugenio Barba and his Odin Teatret, who also participated in the encounter.

In Third Theatre poetics, actors are active generators of meaning through embodied practices, as Turner and Campbell argue in a book that presents Yuyachkani as one of four international case studies of this movement. As they write, the development of performance material "is often characterized in Third Theatre by work on *scores*: repeatable, refined sequences of physical and vocal actions, developed by the actor incorporating texts, songs and work with costumes and objects" (155). Ileana Diéguez calls this non-textual-based approach to the production of semantic material for performance the "dramaturgy of the actor"[15] (*Escenarios* 71), a kind of scenic *écriture*,[16] which comes from the actors' very improvisations and findings, as described above by Turner and Campbell. Rubio, for his part, defines dramaturgy in terms that deemphasize the role of the written text, as "the combination of elements that shape a theatrical spectacle, taking into account the spatio-temporal relationship between the stage and the audience" (Rubio 2001: 51, my translation).

Despite similarities with the European postdramatic tradition, as Diéguez points out, these experimental, actor-based dramaturgies and performance practices in Latin America should be looked at as responses to their own time and space (*Escenarios liminales* [1st ed.] 19–20). In Latin America, she argues, "changes in stage practices, have been closely associated with cultural, political, and economic processes that have taken place in each country and modified the lives of theater practitioners" (*Escenarios liminales*, 2nd ed., 68).[17] Accordingly, Latin American theater scholars like Diéguez[18] and directors like Miguel Rubio himself, who in various publications has theorized about his own group's trajectory and the broader context of Latin American experimental dramaturgies, have developed their own vocabulary to talk about these dramaturgical and performance practices, which can be situated within the global frames of postdramatic and Third Theatre, but are also specific to their own development over fifty years of uninterrupted work. In particular, Yuyachkani draws from traditional Peruvian religious and festive performance traditions from different indigenous communities, especially evidenced in their use of masks, costumes, and the training of the actor as a dancer.[19] In Yuyachkani's "liminal" practice (to use Diéguez's concept), a script, if one is to be used, is brought into the creative process only after the practitioners have gone through the creation of those embodied scores that Turner and Campbell refer to, which Rubio conceptualizes variously throughout his writings as "sensorial accumulation" and a process of "creation" and "recreation."

Considering these performance traditions and approaches to the production of meaning on the stage is necessary for a better understanding of Yuyachkani's *Antígona*. Particularly, it helps understand the process of scenic *écriture* Ralli went through before bringing in Watanabe as a collaborator. Ralli and Rubio invited Watanabe to write a script that would be more fitting than Sophocles' text to the performance materials they had created after a year of working on their own "sensorial accumulation." The ways in which this scenic *écriture* left its traces in Watanabe's writing are not always perceptible, nor are the ways in which the poems, which Watanabe brought to each rehearsal, modified Ralli's own dramaturgy. Yet there is one telling example that serves to illustrate the bidirectional path of the collaboration. In the last scene/poem (XXII), the mortuary mask of Polinices appears in a stage quotation: after the Narradora has just revealed her identity and addresses the spirit of Antígona, the stage quotation says: "She unfastens a bundle and reveals Polinices' mortuary mask" (see Figure 1.1).[20] A few lines later, the Narradora makes an explicit mention of the mask she is holding in her hands when she says:

> Dear sister, look:
> > *this is the face of our brother*, as it was before the dogs
> > and the vultures, and putrefaction,
> > and these late libations are from my little spirit full with remorse.
> (*Ant.* XXII, emphasis mine)

FIGURE 1.1 Teresa Ralli in the role of the Narradora/Ismene, holding the mortuary mask of Polinices in her hands. Photograph by Elsa Estremadoyro. *Source*: Yuyachkani's archive.

The mask made its way into the text out of the encounters of actress and poet in the rehearsal room. As Ralli recounts in *El desmontaje de Antígona*:

> When I first began the process and was working with many objects, I had brought in a white mask, maybe because of the connection to Greek theater. It was a face that made an impact on me. I brought the mask with me every day, enfolded it in a white gauze, and left it there

on the side of the stage. Now and then I would pick it up and use it for some dialogue exercises, to unfold into two characters. Eventually, the mask was left out of the process. But, to our great surprise, one day the mask showed up in one of the poems that Watanabe brought us: it was Polinices' mortuary mask.[21]

The trajectory of the mask, from a prop proposed first by the actress in the process of sensorial accumulation, then discarded by her in rehearsals but taken up by the writer, who inscribed it back in the text, in the form of a stage quotation, thus also putting it back on the stage, this trajectory, I say, clearly shows the bidirectional nature of the collaborative process.

The ways in which the artists mutually influenced each other's work destabilizes notions of authorship, so that *Antígona* stands as a multi-layered and manifold writing, as much Ralli's scenic *écriture* as Watanabe's literary production. This inserts the text, not only the performance, into contemporary and postmodern authorial practices, where notions of authorship are constantly destabilized. It ties in with Roland Barthes's idea that "there is no other time than that of the enunciation and every text is eternally written *here and now*" (*Image Music Text* 145, emphasis original). The "here and now" of authorial enunciation in *Antígona*, with its two authors, moves between the stage and the page (and then of course— as Barthes also argued—shifts to the here and now of spectators and readers).

The decision to cast the character of Ismene as a narrator and witness who recounts the events of the tragedy to the audience is also the result of the collaborative process. In an interview with Diana Taylor, Rubio asserts that telling the tragedy from the point of view of the surviving sister directly spoke to the ongoing struggles in Peru.[22] As the CVR would write in the opening lines of its *Final Report*, Peruvians suffered a double outrage: "that of massive murder, disappearance and torture; and that of indolence, incompetence and indifference of those who could have stopped this humanitarian catastrophe but didn't" (*Informe Final* I: 11). Accordingly, the artists concerned themselves not only with the mothers, sisters, daughters, and wives, who like Antigone in the myth sought justice for the dead bodies of their loved ones, but also with the role of Peruvian society as a silent, passive, and complicit witness of a decades long catastrophe. This emphasis on the role of the witness, as has been frequently noted in the scholarship, makes *Antígona* different from other Latin American recreations of the myth, where, as Moira Fradinger argues, it is the role of motherhood that has been frequently emphasized ("Demanding the Political"). Watanabe, on his part, used his experience as a screenwriter for film to give to the text the cinematic turn, whereby the identity of the Narradora is only revealed at the very end. The double authorship is also visible in the publication of the script. On the opening night of Ralli's performance in January 2000 at Casa Yuyachkani, the company's rehearsal space and theater house in Lima, Watanabe's *Antígona* was also released in book form, published by Yuyachkani itself and the Comisión de Derechos Humanos (Commission for Human Rights).[23] The simultaneity of opening night and book release underscores the alignment of published text and performance, which mirrored each other identically. In fact, the covers of that first edition of the book and of the opening night's program are almost indistinguishable, except that on the cover of the book Watanabe alone appears as the author, while only Yuyachkani appears on the performance program (see Figures 1.2 and 1.3). They attribute authorship to each individual artist according to the medium, thus calling attention to their different agencies over the text. The two almost identical covers align both *écritures* with one another; at the same time, the different authorial attributions underscore how, to say it with Simon Perris, "reading and spectating are related, distinct aesthetic experiences" (184).[24]

Yet Watanabe's published text and Ralli's performance have become more distinct in the last two decades. A few years after the opening night in 2000, the actress complemented her staging of *Antígona* with two other public texts, authored solely by her: one is the artist talk *El desmontaje de Antígona*, which Ralli now often presents after the show or even by itself;[25] the other is a written version of the talk, published (originally in English) as "Fragments of Memory." These two authorial interventions by Ralli epitomize what we may call with Gerard Genette, "public authorial epitexts." As defined by Genette, an epitext is "any paratextual element not materially appended to the text within the same volume but circulating, as it were, freely, in a virtually limitless physical and social space" (*Paratexts* 344). The epitext is a "public authorial" one when, as in Ralli's case, the author herself produces it as an appendage directed towards a public audience or readership (351–2). Ralli's two public authorial epitexts do not focus as much on textual aspects of the script but rather on her own dramaturgical process of scenic *écriture*. They give rich behind the scenes information that a reader or spectator of the play would not necessarily have simply from reading or spectating the play, generating yet another textual layer that complicates and expands its semantics. By recounting the creative process and exposing the artist's motivations, intentions, and vital experiences—making it clear that *Antígona* means to address the violent and traumatic circumstances experienced in Peru from 1980 to 2000—these

FIGURE 1.2 Cover of the original edition of *Antígona*, published jointly by Yuyachkani and Comisión de Derechos Humanos and released on the opening night of Ralli's performance in the theater house of Yuyachkani in Lima in January, 2000.

FIGURE 1.3 Cover of the program for the opening night of Ralli's *Antígona* in the theater house of Yuyachkani in Lima in January, 2000.

two epitexts intervene decisively in the reception and interpretation of *Antígona*.[26] They especially inscribe *Antígona* onto Ralli's body as the original performer and co-creator, who uses her body as a locus to give voice to the experience of real historical women (Ralli, "Fragments" 361), and they inscribe the text onto Peru's landscape at the turn of the century, the geographical and historical context from which it emerged.[27] Ralli's gestures of inscription ought to be considered within two broader frames. On the one hand, there is Yuyachkani's decades-long work on cultural and social memory in Peru.[28] As Katherine Nigh has noted, Yuyachkani's "performances often explore the cultural divides that contributed to the devastating violence within Peru, a recurrent theme in their performances even before the civil war began" (145). Thus, this performance and texts participate of and signify within a broader web of performances and texts produced by the theater group around armed violence in their country as well as their members' activist work with different marginalized communities. On the other hand, this corporeal and geopolitical inscription of *Antígona* also evokes, and thus also means within, the context of a long history of politically engaged uses of Sophocles' *Antigone*, which transcends national borders and is simultaneously global and specifically Latin American (as we will see in the next section).[29]

Yet, something that tends to go unnoticed is that in contrast to Ralli's inscriptional aesthetics, Watanabe's script stands quite uninscribed. Or rather that it lends itself more easily to other kinds of inscriptional gestures. For instance, if we move the text from the contextual assemblage signaled above, grafting it, instead, into a different assemblage—say its relationship to Sophocles' *Antigone*—the fact that the text lacks direct historical references to Peru becomes salient.[30] This lack of inscription is consonant with Watanabe's poetics, as he states in an interview with Ramón Ordaz that he does not believe that poets "have to write literally about what is happening in their social context" (49, my translation). Not marking *Antígona's* inscription onto the Peruvian landscape, the text retains Sophoclean signs as far as the names of the characters, places, and gods go, as well as in respect to the main events of the plot. And so, what distinguishes this *Antígona* is not only its focus on the witnessing role of Ismene but also the layered nature of collaborative writing that resulted in two closely related yet distinct artistic products. Furthermore, by virtue of its publication, the literary text becomes even more distinct from the performance: separate and susceptible to other kinds of analysis, dissemination, and re-performances.[31] By this I do not mean that the published text is free from what Edward Said calls "worldliness" or circumstantial reality (*The Word* 34). Rather, I mean that such worldliness is contradictory and even paradoxical: the historical circumstances of emergence of the text, never eradicated from its semantic wealth (and always demanding for the critic to render them visible), coexist with other (always historical, but shifting and never fully closed) circumstances of reception and dissemination.[32]

This textual condition becomes even more acute in the event of translation, as translation expands circulation among audiences in linguistic contexts that are very different from that of the original performance and publication, quite literally making it mean differently.[33] Thus, as I present the literary text for the first time in its entirety to Anglophone readers, I am taking the opportunity to invite readers to dwell on these rich differences between Ralli's scenic *écriture* and Watanabe's script. I do not mean this as an exclusionary opposition, nor is it a matter of value. It is not about whether *Antígona* is either fixedly inscribed and localized or not. Much to the contrary, *Antígona*, I believe, is most relevant and exciting because it is both/and, because of its layered writing and the manifold semantics embedded in its history, which I have been intent on singling out. It is our task as readers, students, critics, and interpreters to enjoy the work in its semantic wealth, reading text and performance *beside*. I borrow this concept from Eve Kosofsky Sedgwick, who proposes it in the following terms:

> Beside is an interesting preposition also because there's nothing very dualistic about it; a number of elements may lie alongside one another, though not an infinity of them. Beside permits a spacious agnosticism about several of the linear logics that enforce dualistic thinking: noncontradiction or the law of the excluded middle, cause versus effect, subject versus object. Its interest does not, however, depend on a fantasy of metonymically egalitarian or even pacific relations, as any child knows who's shared a bed with siblings. Beside comprises a wide range of desiring, identifying, representing, repelling, paralleling, differentiating, rivaling, leaning, twisting, mimicking, withdrawing, attracting, aggressing, warping, and other relations. (*Touching Feeling* 8)

Hence, this book touches upon the double (though not dualistic) versions of *Antígona*, including materials and bibliography aimed at fostering a manifold and noncontradictory understanding of it. With this purpose in mind, I have written this extensive introduction to give some important points of entry into the complex aesthetics of this piece. And I have also followed the bilingual text with a reading that draws from different theories and methodologies (discourse analysis, deconstruction, affect theory, postcolonial and decolonial criticism, feminist critique, and classical reception). However, because Ralli's performance and epitexts have been privileged in the scholarship, in the third chapter I focus exclusively on textual aspects of Watanabe's script, which has been thus far disregarded.[34] But I highly encourage readers to watch Ralli's beautiful, delicate, and powerful performance, her lucid and moving artist talk, and to read the scholarship written on her work (and Yuyachkani's).

Antígona, with an accent

As already mentioned, Ralli's and Watanabe's *Antígona* is/are part of a long history of performative and literary engagements with this Greek myth and tragedy in Latin America.[35] So many versions of Sophocles' *Antigone* have been written and produced in the region that some critics have called it "a Latin American tragedy."[36] Moira Fradinger, tracing an erudite map of the long and widespread journeys of this Theban heroine throughout the world, identifies twenty original versions in Latin America before 2010, the year of publication of her article.[37] Theorizing receptions of Antigone in Latin America, elsewhere Fradinger proposes the metaphorical concepts of "cannibalization"[38]—drawing from Oswald de Andrade's *Manifiesto Antropófago*—and "rumination"[39] to signal the status of the Greek tragedy (and Greek culture in general) in Latin America as something that was once external, during colonization, but that has become internal through obsessive revivals of the myth during and after independence processes over the last two centuries.[40] As she argues, "this endless rumination allows us to envision the construction of a corpus of American *Antigones* that engage in regional dialogues with their own internal dynamics" ("Demanding the political" 64). Through these processes of creolization, the myth of Antigone has become internal to Latin American letters; conversely, I add, through its insisting returns in the continent, Antígona with an accent has come to form part of what we call "Antigone,"[41] "that body of texts produced, disseminated, contested, institutionalized, performed, and criticized over a long period of time by a wide variety of social agents"—to borrow the words David Johnson uses to define "Shakespeare," which apply perfectly here (5).

Two of these Antígonas with an accent are immediately relevant for those interested in Ralli's and Watanabe's. I refrain, however, from generating a grand, overarching narrative where these very different writings can be made coherent with each other. On the contrary, they are a testament to the stark variety of appropriations of this myth, even only in Peru. The first one is *Antígona (A poem in prose)* [1945], by the Peruvian poet Jorge Eduardo Eielson, and the second, *Antígona*, by Peruvian playwright Sarina Helfgott [1964]. Together with Ralli's and Watanabe's, Eielson's and Helfgott's are the three main engagements with "Antigone" in Peru, each

showing unique aesthetic and political concerns and thus frustrating any
effort to establish generalizations about "Peruvian" Antígonas.[42]

Jorge Eduardo Eielson (Lima, 1924–Milan, 2006) was a symbolist and
avant-garde Peruvian poet, very influential in modern Peruvian letters.[43]
His *Antígona (A poem in prose)* was published in 1945 and is set in the destroyed landscape of Europe in the immediate aftermath of World War
II. Like Watanabe's, it is written in the form of a long poem (though in
prose, as the subtitle announces) divided into sections and combines monologue with narrative elements; unlike Watanabe's, it was not written for
the stage. Yet, it should be noted that Eielson's version of "Antigone" is set
in Europe (where Eielson in fact spent most of his life and died). His text
presents itself as a European version and thus disavows its creole status—
that process of "rumination" whereby the ancient text is re-situated as
pertaining to Latin American mythology. And in this it differs substan-
tially from Watanabe's aesthetics. Watanabe certainly does not precisely
fashion its text as "Peruvian" in any obvious way, that is, he offers no
allusions to Peru, nor does he "Peruvianize" the Sophoclean plot by such
means as changing the names of characters, places, and time of the action.
Yet his text is neither intent on doing the opposite; it does not try to *not*
be Peruvian—as one might argue of Eielson's. Despite these significant
aesthetic differences, Watanabe's and Ralli's and Eieslon's Antígonas share
in common their being, in Olga Kekis' terms, "radical re-makings." They
"use history, myth and culture as a source to draw upon in order to create
dramas which stage and critique crises of our own era" (3).

Sarina Helfgott's *Antígona* was staged in 1964 in Lima (but was not published until 2007). The play was staged in the context of another military
suppression of communist guerrilla uprisings, prior to the insurgencies
of Sendero Luminoso and Movimiento Revolucionario Tupac Amaru.[44]
Polyneices' (in this version, Jaime) army is implicitly analogized to that
of the guerrilleros, while Ramón (Creon) parallels General Juan Velasco
Alvarado. Despite the implicit denunciation of the military suppression,
the politics of this domestic version of the drama differ greatly from Ralli's
and Watanabe's. This is a conventional play (as opposed to experimental)
adapted to the Peruvian society of the times. The names of the characters are, for example, changed to Hispanic ones that sound similar to the
Greek (Ismene to Elena, Creon to Ramón, Haemon to Hernán), except for
Antígona, which stays the same (at one point, Ramón remarks on the sin-
gularity of the name: "Antígona, Antígona, what a strange name!" 22).[45]
Streamlined to only one act, in this version of the plot Antígona confronts Ramón (Creon) without ever being caught by a guard and confesses

her deed without threat of violence. Ramón reacts furiously at first, but is then moved to pity and, in a surprising twist of the plot that firmly places this version within the tradition of melodrama, kisses her forcefully and confesses his love. Fighting her way out of Ramón's assault, Antígona stabs herself to death. Thus, this version does not quite align itself with Antígona as a victim. Moreover, it considerably softens the Creon figure by presenting Ramón as merciful (a mercy that is perversely mixed with sexual desire), even giving Antígona the chance to repent (24) and never actually punishing her, as she kills herself before he exercises punishment. Furthermore, the play closes with Ramón himself mourning Antígona. This conventional melodrama, which considerably dilutes the violence of the Greek, is precisely the kind of bourgeois theatrical scene, aligned with hegemonic cultures and bourgeois values, which Yuyachkani's theatrical practice reacted against.[46] Ralli's *Antígona*, with its enactment of social memory and engagement with communities affected by the violence, becomes more unique when understood against this background.

José Watanabe's poetics of embodiment

As a collaboration, *Antígona* is atypical within the corpus of Watanabe's poetry. It is, in fact, the only theatrical text he ever wrote—though he had plenty of experience writing scripts for television and film, which is how he made a living for most of his life. Nonetheless, many characteristics of his poetics can be observed in the dramatic text, and his style is undeniable, despite Ralli's significant input, as noted above. Hence, a brief consideration of Watanabe's poetics is warranted in order to give readers yet another point of entry into the appreciation of this work as a literary artifact. Not widely known and seldom translated in the Anglophone world, Watanabe's work merits particular attention.[47]

Watanabe's poetics are characterized by solemnity and an attentive gaze to the simple objects of daily life.[48] He thought that poetry was born out of life's vulgarity [sic] and the surprise we feel whenever that vulgarity becomes suddenly elevated [sic].[49] As Esperanza López Prada has noted: "From a delicate and tiny detail, Watanabe's poem tells a fable, a mythology of origins in miniature" concerning things like "mud, fire, smoke, domestic animals, the unrefined quality of the mother, the din in the orchard, the agricultural duties, the needs of the body."[50] Describing himself as a "realist" and a "naturalist,"[51] his poetry is interested in keeping close to the ground, a concern he brings to his writing of *Antígona*, as we will see in the third chapter.

Yet, coexisting with his earth-bound gaze, one finds in his poems a tendency towards the transcendental. Watanabe himself confessed his preoccupation with transcendence in an interview with Javier Rodríguez:

> Another concern of mine, of a "religious order" so to speak, is transcendence. I'm intrigued by the idea—and I don't know when it started—of transcending the world. Maybe it's some Japanese principle that I involuntary learned from my migrant father, and the idea fascinated me. Because after death I wouldn't like to disappear but to be integrated into something bigger than me, which will last more than me and through which I, somehow, will transcend.[52]

This transcendental inclination can be linked to a search for universals and a taste for parables. In the Introduction to an anthology of Watanabe's poems, accurately named *Elogio del refrenamiento* (A Eulogy of Restraint), Eduardo Chirinos says that Watanabe's readers get the feeling "of being participants in a meditative gaze that knows how to extract from everyday facts their hidden condition of universal parables" (10). In another interview, Watanabe mentions to Andrea Jeftanovic that he believes that "every poem moves towards the parable."[53] And such inclination can be seen in the strong presence of narrative in Watanabe's poems, something that we see in *Antígona* as well, which is, in addition to a performance script, a narrative collection of poems.[54] His taste for parables also informs the final twist of the text, with the revelation of the Narradora's identity, which points to the role of the citizen-witness, both within and outside the poem. As he says in the interview with Rabí do Carmo, "generally towards the end [of the poem] I look for the effect of the parable, to put it like this, the effect of something that alludes to what is beyond the poem itself."

But Watanabe never stays on high, always coming back to matter; as he put it, "the first fatherland is the body."[55] This poet, who keeps his eyes fixed on the realities of embodied life, pays close attention to the movements of the flesh, to the bodily experience of life and death. As López Prada observes, commenting on the epigraph to a book tellingly named *Cosas del cuerpo* (Bodily Matters), "following Martial's advice,[56] Watanabe tries never to forget this flesh that inhabits us," and she adds: "poetry extracts from [flesh] its best metaphors, in as much as poetry is, at the same time, an *incarnation*."[57] Aligned with this "incarnation" in Watanabe's poetry is attention towards death and the experience of bodily dissolution. As the poet puts it in an unpublished, unsigned interview found in his archive:

I am aware [that there is a certain need to be dissolved into nature in my poetry], but that comes mostly from fear, from the fear of death. When I was ill, I had the strange idea of dissolving into something else without going through the transition of dying, without going through physical death.

In fact, this appears in one of Antígona's monologues, when already inside her prison/cave/tomb she wants to enter "light … and dissolve in its nimble quality," exclaiming, "Oh, if only I could take that road, that quick gate, that short path" (XIX).

All the above-signaled features of Watanabe's poetics can be observed in *Antígona*. Written in a limpid verse, with clear images and sober, accessible, language, the text keeps its feet on the ground and meditates on human finitude and transcendence while carefully painting bodily affects.

Finally, a word must be said about Watanabe's attitude regarding the role of poetry in politics (and vice versa). As can be gathered from multiple statements in interviews, Watanabe did not believe that poetry had any political leverage. He distanced himself from the views of some of his contemporaries, especially the poets linked to the magazine *Hora Cero* (Zero Hour) who, as he says in the interview with Jeftanovic, "had an enormous faith in poetry even as a force for social change." This is remarkable when thinking about his *Antígona*, because it stands in stark contrast, if not opposition, to Yuyachkani's engaged and overtly political poetics. There is a tension at the interior of this collaboration which is, in turn, also reflected in the ways in which it has been received by scholars and critics. In spite of Watanabe's concern for beauty and aesthetics, interpretations generally highlight the political aspects of *Antígona* and Yuyachkani's political work with it.

In contrast to the belief in the political power of poetry, Watanabe cared more for poetry's affective work. He hoped his poems would conjure up beauty and pleasure, which he considered a form of solidarity. As he says in an unpublished interview, "I think I write for the sake of solidarity," and he adds, "giving me pleasure is also a form of expressing solidarity with me."[58] Moreover, it was important for him that the poem could grant anyone access to pleasure, that it was accessible. In his poetics, these three things (solidarity with the reader, pleasure, and accessibility) are closely interconnected.[59] In the same unpublished interview mentioned above, he recounts how he considered Vallejo a source of support, because reading Vallejo's poems gave him pleasure, and he states that he would like his poems to do that for his readers. "My responsibility," he says in another interview, "is to give the world an object that aims at being beautiful" (Rabi do Carmo 1).

This poetic stance is particularly explicit in the poem "Razón de las parábolas" (The rationale of parables), which explores poetry's capacity to speak to everyone, with special attention to haptics and words' affective qualities. The poem is a poetics of sorts and is thus a fitting way to close this section:

> The Word,
> being as it is divine, is pronounced
> with a human tongue,
> an ephemeral tongue, yet touched
> by a grace: the parable,
> that little history
> guarding a serene angst: being everyone's. (Watanabe, *Poesía completa*
> 311, my translation)

About this book and translation

In the summer of 2014, I participated in Yuyachkani's International Open Laboratory, an international theater workshop organized and hosted by the group every summer in their theater and rehearsal space in Lima, Casa Yuyachkani. Two of the pieces the company presented as part of the workshop were Ralli's *Antígona* and "El desmontaje de Antígona." Coincidentally, I was working on my own version of Sophocles' *Antigone* at the time, while pursuing graduate studies in Classics at the City University of New York. Naturally, I was drawn to Ralli's work and wrote a paper on her *Antígona*, which I presented at a graduate student conference in Oxford in 2015. I realized that the play was little known among classicists specializing in reception studies; the most influential articles were penned by scholars of modern performance, with none written by a classicist;[60] furthermore, only excerpts of the play were available in English translation.[61] Hence, I decided to take on the task of translating the entire play.

In addition to calling attention to *Antígona*'s history of composition and to its semantic expansiveness, the feminist, decolonial, and affective thoughts that inform my thinking make it necessary to signal that reading also involves an attentiveness to the many artifacts framing and standing *beside* any published work—what Genette has called "paratexts" and "epitexts."[62] Apart from my own paratextual essays in this book, the most obvious ones include the many texts already published on this *Antígona*, which may shape how readers receive it, as well as Ralli's own epitexts, to which I referred above. Less obvious framing elements are, for instance, my own name on the cover, which suggests that the translator is not Anglophone, at least not by descent, and the expectations (high or low) or even anxieties that finding such a name on the cover might produce in readers. The cover also presents a title, *Antígona*, which immediately sends readers to a Greek myth. And there is even a subtitle, "A free version of Sophocles' tragedy," inserting this book in a long chain of receptions of the Sophoclean text and making it obviously relevant to the discipline of classical receptions studies, which, broadly speaking, refers to studies of engagements by post-classical authors, readers, and audiences with works of art produced in ancient Greece and Rome. There is also the editorial series in which this book is being published, called "Classics and the Postcolonial," which already frames this text as having something to do with the academic discipline of Classics (and its common associations with the Western canon and the so-called "high literature") as well as a postcolonial approach to translation and criticism (and its associations with critical approaches to that very canon and to the co-opting of certain literatures by elites).

Finally, I also call attention to the fact that translation implies a change of the text's positionality, a change in readership, and—in tune with current scholarly agreement that meaning takes place at the moment of reception—that this change in readership must also cause a recalibration of what we mean by "the context of the text." As a translator, my intention has been to allow for difference in the receiving language (English), something that happens both intentionally and unintentionally,[63] since I am not a native speaker of English but of Spanish—though Spanish, in my country, is already highly inflected by English. English is my second language, which I mastered reluctantly as a citizen of a US colony. My way of speaking and writing it (with a regional accent)[64] will always have a remainder, a certain quality that is not fully assimilated.[65] This notion of a remainder from the source language in the receiving one has been conceptualized as something that always happens in translation, even when the translator is a native speaker of the receiving language. As Lawrence Venuti proposes: "translating is always ideological because it releases a *domestic remainder*, an inscription of values, beliefs, and representations linked to historical moments and social positions in the receiving situation" (*Translation Changes* 28, emphasis mine). However, in my case, this ideological aspect is even more intense, for I am not quite "domestic" in relationship to the receiving language into which I myself am translating. English is, to use Yazemin Yildiz's postmonolingual concept, my "motherless tongue," and so the remainder is exponential, for it is *undomestic*. Moreover, in my daring to "own" English, my *undomestic* politics are at work: I speak to English-language readers in their own language, where I am not fully at home, even when such an equality remains an impossibility in the world outside of these pages. I am enacting a radical equality as *possible* in this limited space of hospitality,[66] claiming, from my (heavily disciplined and quite privileged, but still) minoritarian and "vernacular" linguistic situation,[67] an (un)belonging to what Edward Said has called "a noncoercive human community" (*The World* 247).

Notes

1 My translation from https://envivo.granteatronacional.pe/video/yuyachkani-antigona, here and elsewhere.

2 Ralli used Ignacio Errandonea's translation, the same that Watanabe then used to write his version. As Ralli told me in an email, she lent her copy of the book to the poet.

3 In 1984, another insurgent organization added to the conflict, the Movimiento Revolucionario Tupac Amaru. This movement was not as powerful and deadly as Shining Path and played a considerably smaller role in the armed conflict. For example, according to the *Final Report*, it was responsible for 1.5% of the deaths, whereas Shining Path was responsible for 53.68%; see Comisión de la Verdad y Reconciliación (CVR), *Informe Final*, vol. I. However, Tupac Amaru was responsible for one of the acts of terrorism that brought the violence directly into Lima, making *limeños* (citizens of Lima) aware of a conflict that for the most part had taken place in the highlands. In 1996, the movement seized the Japanese Embassy and took hostages for four and a half months. This violent episode had an important impact on Ralli, since she happened to live right across the street from the Embassy and witnessed from her window the development of the events. In "Fragments," she explicitly links this experience to her interpretation of *Antígona* (359–60).

4 A category of the undead common in Latin American dictatorships during the Cold War and after, *desaparecidos* ("disappeared") refers to people who were taken by force and never appeared again. No information was ever given about what happened to them, and their families could never confirm their deaths.

5 The Peruvian Truth and Reconciliation Commission gave the specific figure of 69,280 as an estimate for the dead and disappeared based on statistical equations used in Guatemala and Kosovo. The range is between 61,007 and 77,552. See Comisión de la Verdad y Reconciliación (CVR), *Informe final*, annex 2, 13. The numbers for widows and children come from CVR, *Hatun Willakuy* 385; on internal refugees see CVR, *Hatun Willakuy* 386. Readers interested in learning more about Sendero Luminoso and the conditions that gave way to its insurgency might find Carlos Iván Degregori and Stern useful; see also Starn et al.

6 For Fujimori's neoliberal project, see Burt, ch.8, and Bowen. Chauca analyzes the imbrications of armed violence, neoliberal reforms, and religious fanaticism during Fujimori's regime, through the lens of two novels: Mario Bellatín's *Poeta Ciego* (Blind Poet) and José B. Adolph's *Un ejército de locos* (An army of madmen), with relevant sources.

7 Before the *Final Report* was published, the official number of fatal victims sustained by the government had been 25,000 (a huge miscalculation when compared to the more than 60,000 reported by the Commission for Truth and Reconciliation), see Degregori and Stern 181. For Fujimori's culture of oblivion see Bowen, especially ch.8.

8 See Degregori and Stern 178.

9 See also Rubio *El cuerpo ausente* 55–8 and 62–73.

10 See Rubio *Notas sobre teatro* 76–77; and the interview with Diana Taylor: https://hdl.handle.net/2333.1/z8w9gmh6.

11 Founded in 1971, Yuyachkani has become the most prominent theater group in Peru and one of the most original and important in Latin America. Over the past fifty years, their work has continuously engaged with issues of social memory and the racial inequalities of modern Peru. Much has been written about Yuyachkani's work on social memory, both in general and in the specific case of Ralli's *Antígona*: Lambright "Woman, Body and Memory;" Martínez Tabares; Taylor "Staging Social Memory;" A'ness; Persino; Garza; Milton; Nigh; Robles Moreno "Yo soy la hermana" and "Making Memory;" Lerner Febres; Dajes; and Turner and Campbell.

12 Richard Schechner and Eugenio Barba, before Lehman, had already differentiated between, on the one hand, a traditional form of theater that takes a previously written text as a point of departure (a mise en scène) and, on the other hand, the "new theater" that creates a "performance text" through a collaborative process of actors and director, denying the hierarchical position of the written word over the body. See Lehman 85ff.

13 See Chapter 1 in Turner and Campbell. There is an overlap between Lehman's and Barba's theories. Many practitioners of what Lehman calls "postdramatic" theater—like Richard Foreman, Robert Wilson, and Tadashi Suzuki—Barba considered the "second theatre" (see Watson 201).

14 Miguel Rubio recognizes Brecht and Eugenio Barba as important interlocutors but considers other Latin American directors as his most important influencers and teachers, like the Colombians Santiago García and Enrique Buenaventura, pioneers in the practice of "creación colectiva" or "device theater" in Latin America; the Brazilian Osvaldo Dragún; and Puerto Rican Rosa Luisa Márquez, among others (see the interview conducted by Taylor quoted above https://hdl.handle.net/2333.1/z8w9gmh6 and Rubio *Raíces y semillas* 9).

15 Rubio also employed this term frequently in the workshop I took with Yuyachkani in 2014, but it does not appear in the written pieces he has published thus far.

16 I am borrowing the term "scenic écriture" from Lehman, who uses it to describe Klaus Michael Grüber's approach to the de-dramatization of texts (see Lehman 74). Ileana Diéguez uses it as well in her theoretical work on Latin American "liminal" theatricalities (*Escenarios* 71–73).

17 This is my translation.

18 Diéguez aligns her theoretical work with that of Lehman but finds his approach insufficient to think "the political charge" of the Latin American kinds of theatricalities that occupy her (see *Escenarios* 49). See also De Toro; and Dubatti.

19 For Yuyachkani's work with Peruvian indigenous theatrical practices, see Rubio *Notas* 1–10. For their Latin American influences, see Rubio *Raíces* Introduction and chapters 3, 5, and 6; Rubio *Notas* 21ff and 55ff; also, Diéguez *Escenarios liminales* (1st ed.) 27–29 and *Escenarios liminales* (2nd ed.) 67–71.

20 Translations of the play are mine, here and elsewhere. See page 5 below.
21 My translation from https://envivo.granteatronacional.pe/video/yuyachkani-antigona.
22 https://hdl.handle.net/2333.1/z8w9gmh6.
23 Later, in 2013, *Antígona* was included in Watanabe's posthumous *Poesía Completa* (Complete Poetry), published in Spain by the press *Pre-Textos*.
24 This quintessential tension, implicit in any dramatic text, namely that, although it is meant to be performed, it will also be read, has been famously formulated by Michael Cacoyannis in the Introduction to his translation of Euripides' *Bacchae*.
25 For instance, in the 2016 international encounter "Mestiza Chile: Festival y Encuentro Internacional de Mujeres en las Artes Escénicas" in Chile, Ralli presented only *El desmontaje de Antígona*. A recording of the talk from 2020 is permanently available at https://envivo.granteatronacional.pe/video/yuyachkani-antigona.
26 In fact, most scholarly interpretations written about the piece, rely heavily on Ralli's epitexts.
27 This closure of meaning and attachment to a specific historical referent is one way in which Yuyachkani's work, though experimental and sharing many of the characteristics of postmodern aesthetics, is embedded in its own cultural context, in which practices that deauthorize the written text and search for embodied modes of signification are not at odds with historical inscription and referentiality. Though this distances Yuyachkani's work from other postmodern practitioners, in fact, Emma Cole argues, looking at European and US American examples, that some of the most important productions of what came to be known as postdramatic theater are quite overtly political. This should be kept in mind in order to avoid an easy polarization of the North (apolitical, avant-garde, experimental, formalistic, aesthetic, high, élite) versus the South (political, engaged, journalistic, more intent on content than form, popular).
28 See Salazar del Alcázar; Taylor "Staging Social Memory;" A'ness; Persino; Garza; Nigh; and Lerner Febres.
29 For global case studies of uses of Antigone in postcolonial/subaltern contexts, see Andújar and Nikoloutsos; Greenwood "Reception Studies;" Macintosh et al.; Hardwick and Gillespie; and Goff *Classics and Colonialism*. For political uses of Antigone in Europe and the United States, see Mee and Foley. Foley *Reimagining Greek Tragedy* covers political uses of other Greek tragedies in twentieth century United States, and one instance of a political use of Antigone in the nineteenth century. Cole calls attention to the political nature of postdramatic European and American theater and to the role that Greek tragedy has played in its development.
30 Naturally, informed Peruvian readers, and readers versed in Shining Path's history, will find allusions where other readers would not. Certainly, the opening line of the play "Today is the first day of the peace," and the invitation that follows shortly after in poem II to "start to forget," rings with the tune of the status quo attitude, promoted by Fujimori's government, to turn the page and leave the past behind. After the capture of the leaders of Shining Path in 1992, as Degregori puts it, "by mid-decade, forgetting appeared to have been imposed. The 1995 Amnesty Law seemed like its consecration" ("The Years We Lived" 174). The Amnesty Law closed all investigations on human right

abuses and left without effect the few sentences that had already been dictated, thus establishing a policy of oblivion. Another notable instance of what could be an obvious allusion for a Peruvian reader or spectator is when Creonte says in poem IX: "the eyes I've sent around the city have seen how they shake their heads and mutter slander." This line could, perhaps, be read as echoing the words of Shining Path's leader Abimael Guzmán, when in 1988 he said in a famous interview published in the newspaper *El Diario* that "the party has a thousand eyes and a thousand ears" (quoted in Chauca 38). The superstitious character of the Mensajero (an addition of Watanabe's to the Sophoclean source) can also be interpreted through a localizing lens, linking it to Peruvian religiosity and the religious fanaticism that took root during the armed conflict (for religious fanaticism in Peru, see Chauca). Yet the fact that allusions can be found does not weaken my point, my emphasis being on how the text carefully avoids *overt and direct* connections that would force a single reading, localizable only in the Peruvian historical reality.

31 For a theoretical discussion of the differences between performance and written text (especially the ephemerality of the former versus the durability of the later) focused on the performance of ancient Greek tragedy, see Fischer-Lichte "Performance as Event."

32 For an extensive discussion of this paradox at the heart of postmodern aesthetics, see Hutcheon, especially ch.5.

33 This essential difference of contexts produced by the translating process (and publication) itself is signaled by Derrida in *L'écriture et la différence* 312. See also Venuti *Translation Changes Everything* 34.

34 See e.g., Taylor "Staging Social Memory;" Lane; Fernández Cozman; A'Ness; Alonso; Robles-Moreno; and Miranda Cancela "Antígona en Perú."

35 The interested reader can find a broad range of references and case studies analyses in: Henao Castro; Andújar and Nikoloutsos; Miranda Cancela "Dioniso en las antillas;" Bosher et al.; Fradinger *varia loca*; and Hualde Pascual.

36 Pianacci's comprehensive study of versions of Sophocles' *Antigone* written in Latin America since the second half of the twentieth century, bears the title *Antígona: una tragedia latinoamericana* (Antigone: A Latin American Tragedy). For a broader account of the presence of classical texts in Latin America since European conquests, see Hualde-Pascual. Not included in Hualde-Pascual is the Mexican Arturo Ripstein's film *Así es la vida* (*Such is life*), screened at the 2000 Cannes Film Festival.

37 For a full list of the titles, see Fradinger "Nomadic Antigone" 20–3. Missing in Fradinger's list is Sarina Helfgott's *Antígona* (Lima, 1964). Other Antígonas published or performed in Latin America after the date of Fradinger's article are Rogelio Orizondo's *Antigonón, un contingente épico* (Cuba, 2013) and Sara Uribe's *Antígona Gonzalez* (Mexico, 2012). For studies of specific plays, see Andújar and Nikoloutsos; Nikoloutsos "Reception of Greek Drama;" see also Brunn *From Tragedy to Ritual*, which includes Ralli's and Watanabe's version.

38 See Fradinger "An Argentine Tradition," "Danbala's Daughter," and "Demanding the Political."

39 See Fradinger "Demanding the Political."

40 For the notion of the "returns" of Antigone in the postmodern world, see the Introduction to Chanter and Kirkland.

41 A good place to start for those interested in familiarizing themselves with the European members of this "body" of "Antigone" is George Steiner's seminal

work, *Antigones*. Good starting places for "Antigone" outside of Western Europe are Mee and Foley; Vasunia; Bosher et al.; Renger and Fan; Andújar and Nikoloutsos; Liapis and Sidiriopoulou; and Greenwood "Reception Studies." A 2013 issue (vol.

5, issue 3) of the *Classical Receptions Journal* on Eastern and Central Europe's literary engagements with classical antiquity is important as this geographical region remains rather unexplored in classical reception studies, yet it focuses on lyric poetry and does not include studies of tragedy.

42 Valle Salazar recounts other engagements by Peruvian authors with Greek tragedy and myth, other than Sophocles' *Antigone*. He notes that Eielson published, also in 1945, *Áyax en el infierno*, a version of Sophocles' *Ajax* in the form of a fable; Vallejo's play "La piedra cansada" (1937) is inspired by the myth of Oedipus; in 1965, Sebastián Salazar Bondy published a comedy based on both of Euripides' Ifigenias, *Ifigenia en el mercado*; in 1969, Alonso Alegría wrote and staged *El cruce sobre el Niágara*, a play based on the myth of Icarus; and *Elogio de la madrastra* (1988), by the Nobel Prize Prize-winning Mario Vargas Llosa, transforms the myth of Hippolytus into a novel (see "Medea, Ifigenia" 189–190). Neither Eielson's nor Helfgott's versions have been translated into English. Gambaro's *Antígona furiosa* was translated by Marguerite Feitlowitz (see bibliography for details).

43 See Fernández Cozman 12. The poem "Intestino" is an "Homage to Eielson" (published posthumously in Watanabe's *Poesía Completa* 451; the poem appears in translation in Novey 126).

44 In the early 1960s, inspired by the Cuban Revolution, two guerrilla organizations—Ejército de Liberación Nacional (National Liberation Army) and Movimiento de Izquierda Revolucionaria (Revolutionary Left Movement)—tried to rebel against Fernando Belaunde's government, but were quickly crushed by the armed forces under General Velasco Alvarado. In 1968, Velasco lead a coup d'état against Belaunde and became military dictator until 1975.

45 All translations from the Spanish are mine. Interestingly, other writers have also commented on Antigone's name as a self-reflexive marker of the Greek source's foreign status with respect to its adaptation. For instance, Femi Osofisan does something similar in his *Tegonni*, when Antigone meets Tegonni's friends (Osofisan 16–7); as Andújar notes, so does Luis Alfaro (*The Greek Trilogy* 6).

46 See Rubio *Notas* and the 2012 interview conducted by Taylor cited above with link.

47 Available translations into English are José Watanabe, *A path through the cane fields*, translated by C.A. de Lomellini and David Tipton; "Excerpts from *Antígona*," translated by Margaret Carson in Taylor and Constantino 365–70; poems translated by John J. Winters in Ricardo González Vigil and John J. Winters 62–7; three poems translated by Idra Novey in Novey 122–7; and three poems translated by Michelle Har Kim in her article "Becoming-Animal in Asian Americas: Ruthanne Lum McCunn's God of Luck and a Watanabean Tryptich (Three poems by José Watanabe)," no pages. A recent volume on Watanabe's poetics (though poorly edited) is a welcome addition to the study of his body of work in English-language scholarship (see Muth et al.).

48 "Since poets lost the status of prophets, our greatest theme is everyday life," he says in the interview with Ordaz (50).

49 See Jeftanovic https://www.academia.edu/26314035/Entrevista_a_Jos%C3%A9_Watanabe_el_ni%C3%B1o_que_rompi%C3%B3_el_jarr%C3%B3n.

50 See López Prada https://elpais.com/diario/2004/05/22/babelia/1085183436_850215.html. All the interviews mentioned here were published in Spanish, all transaltions are mine.

51 See Jeftanovic. For a rhetorical analysis of Watanabe's realist poetics, see López-Pasarín Basabe.

52 https://circulodelectores.pe/entrevista-jose-watanabe-inedita/.

53 See link above.

54 Favela connects Watanabe's predilection for narrative with his taste for parables.

55 Interview with Javier Rodríguez, see link above.

56 Another presence of an ancient "classical" author in Watanabe.

57 See link above, emphasis in the original. In the words of Vargas Canchanya, Watanabe's "anabatic turn" consists in an "avidness for the real," in the adoption of a sort of materialism where natural objects and a social life linked to nature acquire a central value (126).

58 I read this interview with Luis Fernando Jara from 2003 in its unpublished version as I found it in Watanabe's personal archive. Readers can find the reference to the published version in the bibliography at the end of this introduction, however I was unable to get a hold of that published version, despite my efforts.

59 For a reading that connects Watanabe's view of poetry as a source of solidarity with his tendency towards narrative in the poems, see Tania Favela 362ff.

60 See Taylor and Constantino "Teresa Ralli;" Lane; Robles Moreno "Yo soy la hermana" (in Spanish). Recently, the Classics scholar Valle Salazar an article in Spanish where he analyzes Ralli's and Watanabe's *Antígona* alongside other Peruvian engagements with Greek tragedy (see Valle Salazar).

61 Translated by Margaret Carson.

62 For a reflection on "framing" in the field of classical reception studies, see the Introduction to Maarten De Pourcq et al.

63 For a meditation on the work of the unconscious in the act of translation (though it fails to acknowledge the fact that the translator might not be translating into her "mother" tongue, as is my case), see Venuti *Translation Changes*, especially the chapter "The Difference that Translation Makes. The Translator's Unconscious."

64 See Mukherjee.

65 For the notion of "remainder," see Venuti *Translation Changes* 28ff. For the politics of conceiving translation, especially into American English, as assimilation, see Rafael.

66 Ideas of translation as the enacting of different notions of utopia go back to, at least, Goethe, who conceived of translation as a way to achieve identification with a cultural other, and they impregnate most of the theory of translation produced since the nineteenth century. Utopianism is present in Benjamin's very influential envisioning of translation as a version of "linguistic harmony" ("The Task of the Translator" 76–81). More recently, Lawrence Venuti, in an essay called "Translation, community, utopia," develops a notion of translation as fostering a "common understanding with and of the source culture … that in part restores the historical context of the source text" (*Translation Changes* 17). In Venuti's view, translation is a linguistic "zone of contact" that binds heterogeneous communities around a translated text (20ff). What I am claiming here is much more modest, not fully yet a utopia but an active exercise of equality among two hierarchical languages with uneven distributions of cultural, political, and economic capital.

67 I am using the term "vernacular" in the sense given to it by Mukherjee (after John Guillory), as "variant and localized usages of English, not 'parochial' or 'regional'" (147).

Works cited

Alonso, Laura. "La Narración Como Situación Enunciativa y el Predominio Del 'Ethos' en *Antígona* de José Watanabe y el Grupo Yuyachkani." *Latin American Theatre Review*, vol. 44, no. 2, 2011, pp. 55–67.

Andújar, Rosa, editor. *The Greek Trilogy of Luis Alfaro: Electricidad, Oedipus el Rey, Mojada.* Bloomsbury Methuen Drama, 2020.

Andújar, Rosa, and Konstantinos Nikoloutsos, editors. *Greeks and Romans on the Latin American Stage.* E-book, Bloomsbury Academic, 2020, https://2020, 10.5040/9781350125643.

A'ness, Francine. "Resisting Amnesia: Yuyachkani, Performance, and the Postwar Reconstruction of Peru." *Theatre Journal*, vol. 56, no. 3, 2004, pp. 395–414.

Barthes, Rolland. *Image Music Text.* Translated by Stephen Heath, New York, Hill & Wang, 1977.

Benjamin, Walter. "The Task of the Translator," translated by Harry Zohn, *Theories of Translation: An Anthology of Essays from Dryden to Derrida*, edited by Rainer Schulte and John Biguenet, University of Chicago Press, 1992, pp. 71–82.

Bosher, Katherine, et al., editors. *The Oxford Handbook of Greek Drama in the Americas.* E- book, Oxford University Press, 2015. https://10.1093/oxfordhb/9780199661305.001.0001.

Bowen, Sally. *El Expediente Fujimori. Perú y su Presidente (1990–2000).* Lima, Perú Monitor, 2000.

Brunn, Victoria. *From Tragedy to Ritual: Latin American Adaptations of Sophocles' Antigone.* 2009. PhD dissertation. ProQuest Dissertations and Theses.

Burt, Jo-Marie. *Political Violence and the Authoritarian State in Peru: Silencing Civil Society.* Palgrave Macmillan, 2007.

Cacoyannis, Michael, translator. *Euripides. The Bacchae.* New York, Plume, 1982.

Capetinich, Mirna. "La Máscara de Creonte en *Antígona* de Sófocles y *Antígona Furiosa*, de Griselda Gambaro." *Cuadernos de Literatura*, vol. 11, 2004, pp. 21–38.

Carson, Margaret, translator. "Excerpts from *Antígona*." *Holy Terrors: Latin American Women Perform*, Taylor and Constantino, pp. 365–70.

Chanter, Tina, and Sean D. Kirkland. Introduction. *The Returns of Antigone: Interdisciplinary Essays*, edited by Chanter and Kirkland, State University of New York Press, 2014, pp. 1–22.

Chauca, Edward. "Fanatismo en Tiempo de Guerra y Neoliberalismo: *Poeta Ciego* de Mario Bellatín y *Un Ejército de Locos* de José B. Adolph." *Hispanófila*, no. 178, 2016, pp. 37–50.

Chirinos, Eduardo. Prologue. *Elogio del Refrenamiento*, by José Watanabe, Sevilla, Renacimiento, 2003, pp. 9–13.

Cole, Emma. *Postdramatic Tragedies.* Oxford, Oxford University Press, 2019, https://oxford- universitypressscholarship- com.ezproxy.cul.columbia.edu/view/10.1093/oso/9780198817680.001.0001/oso-9780198817680.

Dajes, Talía. "Peru's Living Dead: Spectrality, Untimeliness, and the Internal Armed Conflict." *Romance Quarterly*, vol. 67, no.4, 2020, pp. 181–95.

Degregori, Carlos I. "The Years We Lived in Danger: The Armed Conflict, 1980–1999." *How Difficult It Is to Be God: Shining Path's Politics of War in Peru, 1980–1999*, edited by Carlos Iván Degregori and Steve J. Stern, University of Wisconsin Press, Madison, 2012, pp. 21–36.

De Toro, Fernando. "Elementos Para una Articulación del Teatro Moderno: Teatralidad, Deconstrucción, Postmodernidad." *Quinientos Años de Teatro Latinoamericano: Del Rito a la Postmodernidad*, edited by Sergio Pereira Poza, Santiago de Chile, Bauhaus, 1994, pp. 27–37.

De Pourcq, Martin, et al., editors. *Framing Classical Reception: Different Perspectives on a Developing Field*. E-book, Brill, 2020.

Diéguez, Ileana. *Escenarios Liminales: Teatralidades, Performatividades, Políticas*. Atuel, Ciudad Autónoma de Buenos Aires, 2007.

Diéguez, Ileana. *Escenarios Liminales: Teatralidades, Performatividades, Políticas*. 2nd ed., México, Paso de Gato, 2014.

Dove, Patrick. "In the Wake of Tragedy: Citation, Gesture and Theatricality in Griselda Gambaro's *Antígona furiosa*." Duprey, pp. 42–62.

Dubatti, Jorge, editor. *Nuevo Teatro, Nueva Crítica*. Buenos Aires, Atuel, 2000.

Dunkerley, James. "Latin America since independence." *The Cambridge Companion to Modern Latin American Culture*, edited by John King, Cambridge University Press, 2004, https://doi-org.ezproxy.cul.columbia.edu/10.1017/CCOL0521631513.

Duprey, Jennifer, editor. *Whose Voice is This? Iberian and Latin American Antigones*, special issue of *Hispanic Issues on Line*, vol. 13, 2013.

Eielson, Jorge Eduardo. *Poeta en Lima. Poesía Escrita, Tomo I*, edited by Martha Canfield, Lustra Editores and Sur Anticuaria, Lima, 2015.

Favela Bustillo, Tania. "Un Poeta Narrador." *Desde el Sur*, vol. 8, no. 2, 2016, pp. 353–69.

Fernández-Cozman, Camilo. *Mito, Cuerpo y Modernidad en la Poesía de José Watanabe*. Cuerpo de la metáfora, Lima, 2008.

Fischer-Lichte, Erika. "Performance as Event—Reception as Transformation," Hall and Harrop, pp. 29–42.

Foley, Helene. *Reimagining Greek Tragedy on the American Stage*. University of California Press, 2012, https://california-universitypressscholarship- com.ezproxy.cul.columbia.edu/view/10.1525/california/9780520272446.001.0001/upso-9780520272446.

Fradinger, Moira. "An Argentine Tradition." Mee and Foley, pp. 67–89.

———. "Danbala's Daughter: Félix Morisseau-Leroy's *Antigòn an Kreyòl*," Mee and Foley, pp. 127– 46.

———. "Demanding the Political: *Widows*, or Ariel Dorfman's Antigones." Duprey, pp. 63–81.

———. "Nomadic Antigone." *Feminist Readings of Antigone*, edited by Fanny Söderbäck, e-book, SUNY Press, 2010, pp. 15–23.

Gambaro, Griselda. *Information for Foreigners: Three Plays*. Translated by Marguerite Feitlowitz, Northwestern University Press, 1992.

Garza, Cynthia. "Colliding with Memory. Grupo Cultural Yuyachkani's *Sin Título, Técnica Mixta.*" *Art from a Fractured Past: Memory and Truth Telling in Post-Shining Path's Peru*, edited by Cynthia Milton, e-book, Duke University Press, 2014, pp. 1–34, https://muse.jhu.edu/book/64012 ER.

Genette, Gerard. *Paratexts: Thresholds of Interpretation.* Translated by Jane E. Lewin, E-book, Cambridge University Press, 1997.

Goff, Barbara (ed.). *Classics and Colonialism.* Duckworth, 2005.

Greenwood, Emily. "Reception Studies: The Cultural Mobility of Classics." *Daedalus*, vol. 145, no. 2, 2016, pp. 41–9.

Guillory, John. *Cultural Capital: The Problem with Canon Formation.* University of Chicago Press, 1993.

Hall, Edith, and Stephe Harrop, editors. *Theorizing Performance: Greek Drama, Cultural History, and Critical Practice.* Duckworth, 2010.

Har Kim, Michelle, translator. "Becoming-Animal in Asian Americas: Ruthanne Lum McCunn's God of Luck and a Watanabean Tryptich (Three poems by José Watanabe)." *Transnational Journal of American Studies*, vol. 4, no. 1, 2012.

Hardwick, Lorna, and Carol Gilespie, editors. *Classics in Post-Colonial Worlds.* E-book, Oxford University Press, 2007, https://oxford-universitypressscholarship-com.ezproxy.cul.columbia.edu/view/10.1093/acprof:oso/9780199296101.001.0001/acpro f-9780199296101.

Hatun Willakuy: Versión Abreviada del Informe Final de la Comisión de la Verdad y Reconciliación. Lima, Comisión de Entrega de la Comisión de la Verdad y Reconciliación, 2004.

Helfgott, Sarina. *Teatro de Cámara.* Lima, Linterna de papel, 2007.

Hualde-Pascual, Pilar. "Mito y Tragedia Griega en la Literatura Iberoamericana." *Cuadernos de Filología Clásica. Estudios Griegos e Indoeuropeos*, vol. 22, 2012, pp. 185–222.

Informe Final. Lima, Comisión de Entrega de la Comisión de la Verdad y Reconciliación, 2003.

Hutcheon, Linda. *A Poetics of Postmodernism.* E-book, Routledge, 1988.

Johnson, David. *Shakespeare and South Africa.* Oxford University Press, 1996.

Kekis, Olga. *Hypertheatre. Contemporary Radical Adaptation of Greek Tragedy.* E-book, Routledge, 2019, https://doi-org.ezproxy.cul.columbia.edu/10.4324/9781351253987.

Lambright, Anne. "Woman, Body and Memory: Yuyachkani's Peruvian Antígone." *Feminist Scholarship Review*, vol. XI, no. 1, 2001, pp. 7–11.

Lane, Jill. "*Antígona* and the Modernity of the Dead." *Modern Drama*, vol. 50, no. 4, 2007, pp. 517–31.

Lehman, Hans-Georg. *Postdramatic Theatre.* Translated by Karen Jürs-Munby. E-book, London, Routledge, 2006, https://doi-org.ezproxy.cul.columbia.edu/10.4324/9780203088104.

Lerner Febres, Salomón. "Memory of Violence and Drama in Peru: The Experience of the Truth Commission and Grupo Cultural Yuyackani–Violence and Dehumanization." *International Journal of Transitional Justice*, vol. 14, 2020, pp. 232–41.

Liapis Vayos, and Avra Sidiriopoulou, editors. *Adapting Greek Tragedy: Contemporary Contexts for Ancient Texts.* Cambridge University Press, 2021, https://doi- org.ezproxy.cul.columbia.edu/10.1017/9781316659168.

López-Pasarín Basabe, Alfredo. "Rhetorical Approaches to the Poetry of José Watanabe." Muth et al. pp. 39–114.

López Prada, Esperanza. "Carne Devuelta a la Escritura." *El País*, May 21 2004. www. elpais.com/diario/2004/05/22/babelia/1085183436_850215.html.

Mee, Ericn, and Helene Foley, editors. *Antigone on the Contemporary World Stage.* E-book, Oxford University Press, 2011, https://oxford-universitypressscholarship-com.ezproxy.cul.columbia.edu/view/10.1093/acprof:oso/9780199586196. 001.0001/acpro f-9780199586196.

Miranda Cancela, Elina. "Antígona en Perú, Recepción Clásica y Contemporaneidad." *NEARCO: Revista Electrônica de Antiguedade e Medioevo*, vol. X, no. II, 2018, pp. 15–30.

———. *Dioniso en las antillas*. Madrid, Editorial Verbum, 2020.

Mukherjee, Ankhi. *What Is a Classic? Postcolonial Rewriting and Invention of the Canon.* E- book, Stanford University Press, 2013.

Muth, Randy, et al., editors. *The Poetic Artistry of José Watanabe: Separating the Craft from the Discourse.* E-book, Palgrave Macmillan, 2021.

Nigh, Katherine Jean. "Forgetting to Remember: Performance and Conflict in a Post TRC Peru." *Journal of Dramatic Theory and Criticism*, vol. 27, no. 2, 2013, pp.145–57.

Nikoloutsos, Konstantinos, editor. "*Reception of Greek and Roman Drama in Latin America*," special issue of *Romance Quarterly*, vol. 59, no. 1, 2011.

Novey, Idra, translator. "'The Kung Fu Master' and other poems by José Watanabe." *Review: Literature and Arts of the Americas*, vol. 39, n.1, 2006, pp. 122–27.

Osofisan, Femi. *Tègònni (an African Antigone).* 2nd ed., Concept Publications Limited, Lagos, 2007.

Perris, Simon. "Performance Reception and the 'Textual Twist': Towards a Theory of Literary Reception." Hall and Harrop, pp. 181–91.

Persino, María Silvina. "Cuerpo y Memoria en el Teatro de Los Andes y Yuyachkani." *Gestos*, vol. 22, no. 43, 2007, pp. 87–103.

Pianacci, Rómulo. *Antígona: Una Tragedia Latinoamericana.* Buenos Aires, Losada, 2015.

Ralli, Teresa. "Fragments of Memory," Translated by Margaret Carson, Taylor and Constantino, pp. 355–64.

Rafael, Vicente L. *Motherless Tongues: The Insurgency of Language amid Wars of Translation.* New York, Duke University Press, 2016.

Renger Almut-Barbara, and Xin Fan, editors. *Receptions of Greek and Roman Antiquity in East Asia.* E-book, Brill, 2019.

Robles-Moreno, Leticia. "Making Memory: Patricia Ariza's and Teresa Ralli's Antígonas." *Women Mobilizing Memory*, edited by Ayşe Gül Altınay et al., Columbia University Press, 2019, pp. 346–62, https://doi-org.ezproxy.cul.columbia.edu/10.7312/alti19184-022.

———. "Yo Soy la Hermana Que Fue Maniatada Por el Miedo: Performance Política y Políticas de la Memoria en Antígona, de Yuyachkani." *Hispanic Issues on Line*, vol. 17, no. 17, 2016, pp.126–43.

Rodríguez, Javier. "José Watanabe: 'Belleza es Palabra de Tierra con Ritmo de Agua'." Interview edited by Alexis Iparraguirre, *Círculo de Lectores*, May 23 2020. www.circulodelectores.pe/entrevista-jose-watanabe-inedita/.

Rubio Zapata, Miguel. *El Cuerpo Ausente. Performance Política.* Lima, Grupo Cultural Yuyachkani, 2006.

———. *Notas Sobre Teatro.* Lima, Grupo Cultural Yuyachkani and Minneapolis, University of Minnesota, 2001.

———. *Raíces y Semillas: Maestros y Caminos del Teatro en América Latina.* Lima, Grupo Cultural Yuyachkani, 2011.

Said, Edward. *The World, the Text, and the Critic.* Harvard University Press, 1983.

Salazar del Alcázar, Hugo. *Teatro y Violencia: Una Aproximación al Teatro Peruano de Los 80.* Lima, Centro de Documentación y Video Teatral, 1990.

Söderbäck, Fanny. *Feminist Readings of Antigone.* E-book, State University of New York Press, 2010.

Starn, Orin, et al., editors. *The Peru Reader: History, Culture, Politics.* 2nd ed., E-book, Duke University Press. 2005.

Steiner, George. *Antigones.* Oxford University Press, 1984.

Taylor, Diana. "Rewriting the Classics: *Antígona Furiosa* and the Madres de la Plaza de Mayo." *The Bucknell Review,* vol. 40, no. 2, 1996, pp. 77–93.

———. "Staging Social Memory: Yuyachkani." *Psychoanalysis and Performance,* edited by Patrick Campbell and Adrian Kear, e-book, London, Routledge, 2001.

Taylor, Diana, and Roselyn Constantino, editors. *Holy Terrors: Latin American Women Perform.* E-book, Duke University Press, 2003, https://doi- org. ezproxy.cul.columbia.edu/10.1215/9780822385325.

Taylor, Diana, and Rosalyn Constantino. "Teresa Ralli." Taylor and Constantino, pp. 353–4.

Turner, Jane, and Patrick Campbell. *A Poetics of Third Theatre: Performer Training, Dramaturgy, Cultural Action.* Routledge, 2021, https://doi- org.ezproxy.cul.columbia.edu/10.4324/9781315276311.

Valle Salazar, Luca. "Medea, Ifigenia, Antigone en Peru." *Futuro Classico,* vol. 6, 2020, pp. 181–226.

Vargas Canchanya, Martín. "El silencio de la Escritura. Tres Salidas a la Crisis del Poema en Tres textos de Emilio Adolfo Westphalen, Jorge Eduardo Eielson y José Watanabe." *Entre Caníbales. Revista de Literatura,* vol. 1, no. 6, 2017, pp. 115–33.

Vasunia, Phiroze. *The Classics and Colonial India.* Oxford University Press, 2013, https://oxford-universitypressscholarship- com.ezproxy.cul.columbia.edu/ view/10.1093/acprof:oso/9780199203239.001.0001/acpro f-9780199203239.

Venuti, Lawrence. *Translation Changes Everything.* E-book, Routledge, 2012, https://doi- org.ezproxy.cul.columbia.edu/10.4324/9780203074428.

Vigil Ricardo González, and John J. Winters. "Fifteen High Points of Twentieth-Century Peruvian Poetry." *World Literature Today,* vol. 77, no. 1, 2003, pp. 62–7.

Watanabe, José. *Antígona. Versión Libre de la Tragedia de Sófocles.* Lima, Yuyachkani and Comisión de Derechos Humanos, 2000.

———. "El Estilo es el Lugar Donde Poso mi Alma: Una Entrevista a José Watanabe." Interview with Rabí Do Carmo, *Revista Bimestral del Centro de Estudios y Promoción del Desarrollo,* 2000. https://www.desco.org.pe/recursos/sites/indice/156/671.pdf.

————. "Despertar la Memoria y el Gesto de Ismene." Interview with Vivian Martínez Tabares. *Revista Conjunto*, vol. 121, 2001, pp. 10–6.

————. *Elogio del Refrenamiento.* Sevilla, Renacimiento, 2003.

————. "José Watanabe: Nuestro Gran tema es la Cotidianidad." Interview with Ramón Ordaz. *Poda*, vol. 1, 2015, pp. 41–52.

————. "José Watanabe: Cuerpo, Patria, Naturaleza." Interview with Luis Fernando Jara, *Les Représentations du Corps dans la Littérature Latino-Américaine*, edited by Nathalie Besse, special issue of *Recherches*, vol. 4, 2010, pp. 261–72.

————. *Poesía Completa.* Madrid, Buenos Aires, and Valencia, Pre-Textos, 2013.

————. "Entrevista a José Watanabe: El Niño que Rompió el Jarrón." Interview by Andrea Jeftanovic, *Academia.edu*, www.academia.edu/26314035/Entrevista_a_José_Watanabe_el_niño_que _rompió_el_jarrón.

Watson, Ian. "The Third Theatre: A Legacy of Independence." *Negotiating Cultures: Eugenio Barba and the Intercultural Debate.* Manchester University Press, 2002, pp. 197–220.

Yildiz, Yazemin. *Beyond the Mother Tongue: The Postmonolingual Condition.* E-book, Fordham University Press, 2011, https://fordham-universitypressscholarship-com.ezproxy.cul.columbia.edu/view/10.5422/fordham/9780823241309.001.0001/upso-9780823241309.

2

ANTÍGONA

A free version of Sophocles' tragedy/ Versión libre de la tragedia de Sófocles

José Watanabe

Translated by Cristina Pérez Díaz

I

NARRADORA

Hoy es el primer día de la paz.
Las armas enemigas aún no han sido recogidas y están
    dispersas
sobre el polvo como ofrendas inútiles.
Qué rápido el viento de la madrugada ha borrado las huellas
    de huida de los argivos.
Cuando la luz es brillante como la de esta mañana, parece que
    el pasado
es más lejano.
Pero no, ellos huyeron apenas anoche, no más noches.
Antes de nuestro último sueño fue el tropel de su desbande.

Vinieron
y se posaron sobre nuestros tejados cual águilas armadas
y pusieron en nuestras siete puertas
siete renombrados capitanes
y nunca acallaron sus siniestros gritos de guerra.

Pero Zeus, que abomina los alardes de la lengua altanera,
estuvo con nosotros.
Acosados por nuestros batallones, corrían por su vida
    aquellos que cantaban
que habían venido a beber nuestra sangre.

No la bebieron y agradezcamos hoy la vida
y el sol
y la paz que es un aire transparente, y empecemos a olvidar.

DOI: 10.4324/9781003150350-2

I

NARRADORA

Today is the first day of the peace.
The enemy's weapons haven't been collected yet and lie
scattered on the ground, like useless offerings.

How quickly the wind of dawn erased the traces of the Argives'
flight.

When the sunlight dazzles as it does this morning, it seems
      that the past
is more distant.
But no, they fled only last night, no more nights ago.
Before our last dream came the chaos of their stampede.

They came
like armed eagles, and landed on our roofs
and stationed at our seven gates
seven renowned captains
and never silenced their sinister calls of war.

But Zeus, who hates the fanfare of a proud tongue,
was favorable.

Hunted by our troops, they ran for their lives
      those who'd cried
that they came to drink our blood.
They didn't, and let's thank today for life
and the sun
and peace, which is a transparent air, and let's start to forget.

II

NARRADORA

Los pastores han llevado las cabras y ovejas
más allá de las colinas de Tebas, adonde el pasto
no esté sucio de sangre.
Volverán cuando todos los muertos de la guerra estén
   enterrados
y nueva yerba crezca sobre los túmulos.

Apúrense enterradores,
junten sabiamente en una misma fosa a nuestros soldados y a
   los enemigos
pues ambos están hechos de la misma carne
y oliscan el aire por igual.

¿Ven ese cadáver sobre la tierra más árida,
tendido perfectamente de perfil?
Se llama Polinices y, aunque semidesnudo,
aún mantiene las brillantes insignias de capitán argivo.

Murió por un juego perverso de los dioses.
Ellos observan las batallas como un espectáculo, ignorando
quién hiere a quién en el fragor del combate
o qué flecha lleva dirección de cuerpo preciso.

Pero en una de las siete puertas,
los dioses sí pusieron voluntad para que se enfrentaran dos
   hombres señalados,
nuestro capitán Etéocles
y el capitán atacante, Polinices.

Ay juego perverso:
los dos guerreros de largas lanzas que quedaron mirándose,
increpándose,
solitarios en sus armaduras fulgurantes, ay juego perverso,
eran nacidos de una misma madre y de igual padre.

El movimiento fue simultáneo: una lanza avanzó y la otra vino
y así la muerte se hizo dos, pero entera en cada hermano.

II

NARRADORA

The shepherds drove the sheep and goats
past the Theban hills, where the grass
isn't dirtied with blood.
They will return when all the dead from the war are buried
and new pastures grow over the graves.

Hasten, gravediggers,
be wise and mingle in one tomb our soldiers
        and the enemies
since both are made of the same flesh
and cause the air to reek just the same.

Do you see that dead body lying perfectly on its side on the dry soil?
His name is Polinices and, though almost nude,
he still wears the shining badge of an Argive captain.

He died in a perverse game of the gods.
They look at battles like spectacles, careless
of who wounds whom in the roar of combat
or which arrow arches towards a precise body.

But at one of the seven gates
the gods willed a quarrel between two
        chosen men,
our captain Etéocles
and the attacking captain, Polinices.

Oh perverse game:
the two warriors, long spears, stood facing each other
spewing reproaches,
both lonely in their dazzling armors—Oh perverse game
born from the same mother and of one father.

The movement was simultaneous: one spear advanced and the other
came forward
and thus death was split, but completed in each brother.

III

NARRADORA

Destino es de los débiles crear señores del poder,
 así como en sueños creamos seres para nuestro miedo, y sólo
 el dormido
los ve, y se angustia.

Pero ahora estoy en vigilia y ver a Creonte me intimida.
 Coronado ayer, es el más reciente rey de Tebas, y sin
 embargo
ya su ceño es fruncido.

Está bajando lentamente los escalones de su palacio y sé que
 no trae en la boca
palabras felices.

CREONTE

Nuestra patria nuevamente es una tierra de sosiego.
Después de las violentas marejadas de la guerra,
las cosas se han asentado y funcionan como originalmente.
Miren alrededor:
el vino está en las ánforas,
los sirvientes sacuden las alfombras en las ventanas,
el amor anida otra vez, y felizmente por igual, en los inmortales
y en los hombres efímeros,
y los muertos de la guerra ya todos están abrigados por la tierra,
excepto uno.

Excepto uno.

El cuerpo de Polinices quedará insepulto, carne
de disputa y hartura de las aves y de los perros voraces.
Porque él, que fue desterrado, vino con los crueles argivos
 dispuesto a ver con placer el fuego consumiendo la ciudad
 de sus padres.
La no tumba para él es mi determinación
porque jamás los malvados recibirán más honra que los justos,
y que así quede pregonado.

III

NARRADORA

It is the fate of the weak to produce masters,
just as in dreams we devise creatures for our fears
    and the sleeper alone
sees them and suffers.

But now I'm awake and seeing Creonte frightens me.
Crowned yesterday, he is the most recent king of Thebes, however
his brow is already furrowed.

He steps slowly down the stairs of his palace and I know he's not
    bringing in his mouth
cheerful words.

CREONTE

Our country is again quiet.
After the violent floods of the war
things have settled and function as they used to.
Look around:
the wine is in the vessels,
the servants beat the rugs outside the windows,
love nestles back, and happily in equal portions, among immortals
and ephemeral men,
and the dead from the war are all covered with earth,
except for one.

Except for one.

Polinices' corpse will remain unburied, meat
of contention and satiation for the birds and voracious dogs.

Because he, an exile, came with the cruel Argives
willing to rejoice as the fire consumed
his parents' town.

The no-tomb for him is my resolution
because never shall the unjust receive more honor than the just,
and let it thus be proclaimed.

Y pregonado también quede el castigo: aquel
que le haga exequias, que le haga duelo o que le cubra con
tierra,
agregará su propia muerte a la del muerto.

Ahora vayamos todos a concluir las honras de su hermano
Etéocles:
dispongan carrozas, caballos, flores, banderas,
y ustedes, capitanes de la guerra, agreguen un mechón de sus
cabellos
para que se consuma con el cuerpo de aquel cuya causa fue la
patria.

Queden así en el olvido los pasados combates
y vayamos a los templos de los dioses en danzas nocturnales,
¡y que Baco sea nuestro guía!

And let the punishment also be proclaimed: he
who fulfills the funerary rites, who mourns or covers him
    with dust,
will add his own death to the dead.

Now let us all go and conclude the honorary rites for his brother
Etéocles:
prepare the carriages, horses, flowers, banners,
and you, the war Captains, offer locks of your hair
which will be consumed with the body of that man whose cause
    was his country.

Let us forget bygone struggles
and go to the temples of the gods with nocturnal dances
and may Bacchus be our guide!

IV

NARRADORA

La muchacha, más niña que mujer, sentada en aquel patio...
qué abatimiento tan serenamente llevado.
Hermana de los dos muertos, del honrado con sepulcro y del
    otro, afrentado sin él,
mira distante nuestro paso. La culpa que sentimos está en
    nosotros, tebanos,
no en la intención de su mirada,
porque nadie, ni el consejero más sabio, se atrevió a refutar la
    orden de Creonte
que es dañosa para nuestra alma.

¿Qué cosas arden en tu corazón, Antígona?
¿Adónde vuela tu resentimiento, muchacha?
¿A Zeus, que ha descargado sobre tu familia cuanto dolor hay
    en el mundo
o al rey que ahora se ensaña con tu hermano?

ANTÍGONA

Un cetro, un trono, y venias, muchas venias alrededor
están con Creonte.
Oh rey, no necesitabas mucho para hablar con voz de tirano.
Nadie conoce el verdadero corazón de un hombre hasta no
    verle en el poder.

Antes de la guerra pasaba silbando por este jardín, acariciaba
mi cabeza de sobrina
y luego se perdía por el soleado atrio. Era otro sol
y yo era otra sobrina.

            Ese mismo hombre ordena ahora que me regocije con la
                Victoria
y ponga en olvido al insepulto Polinices
como si no fuera mi hermano.
¿Cómo entrar danzando y cantando en los templos
si en la colina más dura hay un cuerpo sin enterramiento?
¿Cómo brindar, borrando de mis ojos lo que no ven
pero que ciertamente es?

Es un cadáver cercado por guardias, vigilado día y noche
para que ni siquiera el viento le cubra con tierra.

IV

NARRADORA

The girl, more child than woman, sitting on that patio...
what grief, serenely borne!
The sister of the two dead, one honored with a tomb and the
    other, disgraced without it,
she watches from a distance as we pass. The guilt we suffer is within
    us, Thebans,
not in the intention of her gaze, because no one,
not even the wisest of counselors, dared to defy
    Creonte's order,
harmful to our soul.

What blazes in your heart, Antígona?
Where does your sorrow fly, girl?
To Zeus, who unleashed upon your family as much pain as exists
    in the world,
or to the king, who now shows no mercy to your brother?

ANTÍGONA

A scepter, a throne, and courtesies too many
pay court to Creonte.
Oh King, you didn't need much to end up speaking like a tyrant.
No one knows the true heart of a man until he is tested in power.

Before the war, he used to walk around this garden, whistling
he'd stroked my head, the head of his niece,
and then disappear into the sunny atrium. It was another sun
and I, another niece.

That same man orders now that I rejoice
    with Victory
and let unburied Polinices dissolve into oblivion
as if he were not my brother.
How am I to enter the temples, dancing and singing,
if there is a corpse lying without burial on the rugged hill?
How to offer libations, rubbing out what my eyes cannot see
but certainly is?

It is a corpse, surrounded by guards, watched night and day
so that not even the wind might cover him with dust.

Pero si eres perro o ave carnicera, puedes llegarte
destazarlo y morder la preciosa carne
del hermano mío.

Hermano mío, pero ya no pariente mío
sino muerto de todos, dime qué debo hacer.

But if you are a dog or a bird of prey, you can
come close and tear him apart and bite the precious flesh
of my brother.

My brother, no longer my kin
but everyone's corpse, tell me what I should do.

V

NARRADORA

Los dioses te hicieron nacer hembra, Antígona.
Poco puedes hacer sino obedecer las leyes, así caigan sobre
   los muertos
como sobre los que vivimos todavía.
Tienes el corazón puesto en cosas ardientes, en deseos
de desobediencia que a otros helarían o convertirían
en estatuas del miedo.

Descansa, deja que el sueño sea apacible tregua
mientras transcurre la larga noche. Duerme.
(Se hace la noche, luego amanece)

V

NARRADORA

It was the gods' will that you were born a female, Antígona.
Little can you do, but obey the laws, should they fall upon the dead
      or upon us, who are still living.
You have your heart set on fiery thoughts, on desires
of disobedience which would cause others to freeze or turn
into statues of fear.

Rest, let dream be a peaceful truce
while the long night passes. Sleep.
(Night falls, then morning breaks)

VI

NARRADORA

Las raudas sandalias del guardia
que viene corriendo por un atajo de las colinas, de tan raudas
parece que apuran la luz del amanecer.

¿Qué mensaje palpita en su lengua, qué noticia
lo demuda en su carrera, qué nueva calamidad guarda
en sus cerradas palabras?

Ya sube los escalones húmedos de palacio,
ya sólo tiene aliento para pedir que lo anuncien ante el rey.

GUARDIA

Qué difícil llegar hasta ti, rey, no por tus alturas en el poder
sino por mi temor de darte el bocado que traigo.

Cuántas veces me he detenido en mi carrera
porque el corazón me decía: "vuélvete, regresa, cuidado,
que apenas dando la noticia, tú mismo la has de pagar".

Con tales pensamientos
el camino corto me ha dado un viaje largo.

Sí, sé que estoy hablando para dilatar el tiempo mío
y sólo logro tu real impaciencia.

Sea entonces la noticia:
anoche alguien ha sepultado a Polinices.

No, no es que el muerto esté acogido bajo la tierra,
sino que le han frotado fino polvo sobre toda la piel.

El alguien inició así el rito del soterramiento,
pero la luz del alba lo hizo huir.

VI

NARRADORA

The swift sandals of the guard,
who takes the shorter path running through the hills, are so swift
    that
they rush morning.

What message palpitates on his tongue, what news
drains his haste, what fresh calamity does he enfold
in sealed words?

Now he walks up the dewy stairs of the palace,
now he has breath only to ask to be announced to the king.

GUARD

How hard it is to reach you, King, not because of the height of your
    power
but due to my fear in bringing this mouthful of news.
How many times I slowed in my haste
as the heart kept saying: "turn around, go back, be careful,
for as soon as you give the message, you'll pay for it."
With these thoughts whirling
a shortcut gave me a longer path.

Yes, I know I'm blithering to prolong my time
and I've earned no more than your regal impatience.
Let the news be, then: Last night someone buried Polinices.

No, it is not that the man is sheltered beneath the earth
but that someone sprinkled fine dust all over his skin.
Someone started the burial rite
but the coming of dawn forced him to run away.

Guardias contra guardias nos hemos culpado,
pero será, te pregunto, ¿negligencia de hombres si el
　　　　　desobediente de tu decreto
fue un dios?
Ese pensamiento silenció de pronto nuestra discusión allá en
　　la colina.
Señor, convendrás que quien llega y huye
deja huellas,
y no había ninguna, ni de rueda ni de pie ni de arañazo de
　　azada.
¿No te dice el corazón, como a nosotros, que el enterrador
　　llegó por el aire
o que no es de visible sustancia humana?

Guard against guard we've accused each other
but, I ask you, would it be human negligence if the rebel
were a god?
That thought silenced, suddenly, our argument, out there on the hill.
Master, you would agree that whoever comes and goes
should leave traces
and there were none, nor of wheel or foot or of a hoe's scratch.
Doesn't your gut tell you, as it tells us, that the burier came by air
or that he is not of visible human substance?

VII

NARRADORA

En la puerta de Bóreas
el viento agita como tristes banderas los andrajos de aquel
    hombre que viene reo.
Culpado avanza
mientras los cumplidores guardias lo apuran con lanzas
y la turba le hace andante ruedo.

Dicen que merodeaba el cadáver de Polinices
y que había tierra en sus uñas.
Ahí tienes, Creonte, al que anoche retó tu orden.

¿Vas a juzgarlo?
Risible juicio, rey, o sainete: ¿Cómo lo harás venir a la cordura
si el hombre tiene la razón trastocada?

Es el loco que hace años pide limosna junto al monumento de
    Anfión.
Hoy, prisionero, grita que en la colina sólo buscaba a su perro.
Sus otras voces
sólo suenan en su cabeza atormentada, en su locura
donde no existen reyes ni héroes ni traidores,
sino sólo un perro.

VII

NARRADORA

At Bóreas gate
the wind rustles, like sad pennants the rags of that man who comes
    accused.
Blamed, he advances
while the dutiful guards prod him with spears
and the crowd forms his walking hem.

They say that he was roaming around Polinices' corpse
and there was soil under his nails.
There he is, Creonte, the one who challenged your order last night.

Are you going to judge him?
Ludicrous judgement, King, or farce: How will you restore sanity to
    his mind
if the man is mad?

He is the fool who has been begging for many years now at
Amphion's monument.
Today, a prisoner, he cries that he was just looking for his dog up on
    the hill.
Other voices
resound in his head, tormented in his madness
where there are no kings, no heroes, no traitors
but only a dog.

VIII

NARRADORA

Yo recuerdo:
las alamedas eran primaverales
y Antígona corría y reía como un pequeño ciervo con sus
    amigas.
El único acontecer trémulo
era la primera sangre menstrual, brillante y limpia,
y el único vaticinio
lo traía el viento al cifrar los vestidos a los cuerpos, y anunciar
así cuerpos plenos y deseables.

Nada presagiaba a la joven sombría que hoy camina sola bajo
    los pinos
y apoya la mejilla en la áspera corteza para que nada en ella
descanse serenamente.

Los dioses de la alameda la miran pasar y ninguno, desde sus
    mármoles,
la consuela.

ANTÍGONA

Oh dioses, pudiendo habernos hecho de cosa invisible o de
    piedra
que no necesitan sepultura
¿por qué nos formaron de materia que se descompone, de
    carne
que no resiste la invisible fuerza de la podredumbre?

Qué impúdico, que obsceno
es acabarse insepulto, mostrando
a los ojos de los vivos blanduras y viscosidades. Tal castigo,
y peor, padece mi hermano
porque también es abasto que desgarran alimañas, buitres
    y perros.

VIII

NARRADORA

I remember:
the groves were in full blossom
and Antígona used to run about with her friends and laugh like a
    little fawn.
The first drops of menstrual blood were the only moment of tremor,
clean and brilliant,
and the only omen
was the wind, as it fitted the dresses to their bodies, announcing
them
ripe and desirable.

Nothing foretold of the somber girl who now
walks alone under the pine trees
and leans her cheek on the rough bark so that nothing in her
may rest calmly.

The gods of the grove look at her
and none, from their marble, console her.

ANTÍGONA

Oh gods, when you could have made us of invisible substance or
    stone
that needs no burial,
why make us of rotting matter, of flesh
that does not resist the invisible force of putrefaction?
How lewd, how shameless

to meet one's end unburied, displaying for the eyes of the living
gelatinous and viscous matter.
    Such punishment
and worse, my brother suffers,
for he is a provision for vermin, vultures,
    and dogs to tear at.

Altos pinos que me vieron pasar cuando yo era niña,
¿divisan a mi hermano? ¿el viento le ha quitado el fino polvo
con que cubrí su desnudez al amanecer?
¿Tendré otra vez valor para burlar la redoblada guardia
o debo resignarme a que su cuerpo, al entrar el otoño,
sea sólo huesos y una mancha oleosa sobre la grava?

No, no me respondan. Hoy toda palabra o murmullo entra en
   mi pesadilla
y la enciende más.

Tall pine trees who saw me walking as a child,
can you see my brother? Did the wind blow away
the fine dust I sprinkled over his naked body at sunrise?
Will I have the courage to mock the doubled guard again
or should I surrender his body to be nothing more than bones
and an oily stain on the gravel at the waking of autumn?

No, do not answer. Today every word or whisper sets foot in
    my nightmare
and kindles it more.

IX

NARRADORA

Era la medianoche
y el palacio de Creonte parecía un barco anclado y seguro.
El viento había amainado
y las antorchas se consumían con llama inmóvil y azul.

Contemplando el edificio, pensé en los modos del poder:
un hombre inmisericorde duerme entre sedas, me dije.

De pronto
en la habitación más alta se encendió una luz y otra luz
y vi a Creonte caminar y caminar turbado. ¿Lo despertó
un mal sueño
o el escozor de la desconfianza que tiembla en la piel de todo
    tirano?

CREONTE

El guardia habló con lengua supersticiosa. No viendo huellas,
él y sus compañeros de simpleza
sospecharon una divinidad intentando sepultar el cadáver de
    Polinices.

¿Qué dios puede tomarse ese trabajo
con alguien que llegó hasta las puertas de la ciudad
                    levantando teas ardientes
dispuesto a incendiar templos, altares y sacros tesoros?

¿O hemos llegado al tiempo en que dioses falsos
enaltecen a los traidores?

No: ahora veo: la simpleza del guardia era fingida
y el dios enterrador era pícaro invento
para ocultar su complicidad pagada.

IX

NARRADORA

It was midnight
and Creonte's palace looked like a ship, safe and anchored.
The wind abated
and the torches burned with a flame, immobile, blue.

Looking at the building, I thought about the modes of power:
there is a man sleeping in merciless silk, I told myself.

Suddenly,
in the highest room a light turned on,
and another,
and I saw Creonte pacing and pacing troubled. Did a bad dream
wake him
or was it the sting of suspicion that shivers in the skin
    of every tyrant?

CREONTE

The guard talked with a superstitious tongue. Not seeing any traces,
he and his foolish mates
suspected a divinity attempting to bury the corpse
    of Polinices.

What god would take on this trouble
for someone who approached the gates of the city with blazing
    torches
    raised
to burn temples, shrines, and sacred treasures?

Or have we come to a time when false gods
exalt traitors?

No: now I see: the foolishness of the guard was a pretence
and the gravedigger-god was a device
to mask the bribe for his complicity.

Hay ciudadanos resentidos porque no ocupan un sitio a mi
    lado.
Ojos que yo envío por toda la ciudad
han visto que a mis espaldas mueven la cabeza y murmuran
    diatribas.
A ellos no les duele el cadáver de la colina, les duele mi poder,
y para minarlo
dejaron caer monedas sobre la palma venal de un guardia.
Sí, la arriesgada y vergonzosa empresa de mi servidor
sólo puede hallar explicación en el lucro.

Y luego quisieron confundirme como al rey ingenuo de las
    fábulas
trocando a un dios con un loco que se arrodilló ante mí
y habló confusas palabras entre llantos y babas.

Poder y traición están en la misma medalla.
El día de mi primer mando tuve mi primera felonía:
desapareció la mascarilla mortuoria de Polinices, aquella
que hice para que el enemigo tuviera un rostro
antes de que bajo el sol, como ordené, perdiera sus facciones.

Ay traidores, tiemblen, porque tampoco bastará la muerte sola
    para ustedes.

Some citizens resent that they don't have a place
    close to me.
The eyes I've sent around the city
have seen how they shake their heads and mutter
    slander.
The corpse on the hill does not hurt them, my power hurts them
    and to weaken it
they let some coins drop into the venal palm of a sentinel.
Indeed, my servant's bold attempt
can only be explained by profit.

And then they wanted to confuse me like an ingenuous
    king from fables,
trading a god for a fool, who knelt down in front of me
and babbled amidst drool and tears.

Power and treason are stamped on the same coin.
The day I gave my first order I was first betrayed:
the funerary mask of Polinices disappeared, the one
I forged to give a face to the enemy
before he lost his traits under the sun, as I commanded.

Oh, traitors, tremble, for you, as well,
death won't be the only punishment.

X

NARRADORA

He visto a Antígona corriendo sigilosa de una columna a otra,
de una esquina a otra
corno escondiéndose de nadie.

Al salir por la puerta Bóreas
su apurado vestido blanco parecía ir solo como una sábana
   volada de un cordel.

La perdí de vista cuando entró en la llanura,
pero en la frente llevaba un pensamiento que la transfiguraba
y la haría más bella en su veloz caminar bajo el sol del
   mediodía.

ANTÍGONA

Polinices, hermano mío, te preguntarás cómo he llegado hasta
   ti.
Todo hombre tiene su arrogancia
y la de los guardias es creer que en hora tan luminosa no
                         puede haber audaces.
Doy gracias también a los vientos del norte
que se rizan en torbellinos y recorren las colinas
levantando columnas de polvo que suben hasta las nubes.
Envuelta en un torbellino he venido. Estoy llena de briznas,
pero el vino del cántaro está limpio.

Cuán malamente te han raspado el polvo
que te puse anteanoche. Quieren para ti la más absoluta
   intemperie,
pero yo he venido a abrir la tierra para ti.

Recibe otra vez sobre tu cuerpo este polvo consagrado
y estas tres libaciones del vino de mi boca, pero en nombre de
   todos.
(La sorprende un guardia)

X

NARRADORA

I've seen Antígona running, furtive, from one pillar to the other,
from one corner to another
as if hiding from an invisible eye.

As she hurried out the Bóreas gate
her dress seemed to move on its own, like a white sheet
    dangling from a clothesline.

I lost sight of her when she entered
the plain carrying a thought that transmuted her face
    and magnified her beauty as she walked swiftly
under the midday sun.

ANTÍGONA

Polinices, my brother, you might wonder how I've made my way to you.
Every man has his arrogance
and as for the sentinels, they trust that in such a dazzling hour
there could be no daring.

I thank the north winds,
eddying and sweeping the hills
they lift columns of dust up to the clouds.
Enveloped in a whirlwind I've come, flecked
with straw, but the wine in my vessel is pure.

How cruelly they scraped away the dust
I sprinkled over your body the night before last.
They wish for you a sky absolutely open, but
I've come to open the earth for you.

Let your body receive again this sacred dust
and these three wine libations from my mouth, but
in the name of all.
(A guard catches her by surprise)

Ser sorprendida era mi riesgo, guardia, pero déjame
que termine de abrir la tierra para que sea madre
y acoja a Polinices como acogió a Etéocles.
Son hermanos irrenunciables, guardia, ya sin facción ni
    contienda
y acaso mutuamente se están llamando.

En tu corazón sabes
que no es bueno que el uno esté abrigado por la tierra
y el otro siga errando,
alma en pena que mira con tristeza o cólera su propio cadáver.

Quiero que toda muerte tenga funeral
y después,
después.
después
olvido.

En tus amarras, guardia, está empezando mi muerte.

Recuerda mi nombre
porque algún día todos dirán que fui la hermana que no le
    faltó al hermano:
me llamo Antígona.

I risked being caught, guard, but let me finish opening
the earth, so that it can be a mother to Polinices
and receive him as she received Etéocles.
They are now inalienable brothers, guard, without faction
    or dispute,
and perhaps mutually they are calling out to each other.

In your heart you know
it is not right that the earth covers one
    while the other wanders,
a suffering soul, watching its carcass with pain or rage.

For every death I want a funeral,
and then,
then,
then,
oblivion.

Caught in your bonds, guard, my death begins.

Remember my name,
because one day everyone will say that I was the sister who did not
fail her brother:
my name is Antígona.

XI

NARRADORA

Gentes de Tebas
que miran y se esconden como monos curiosos,
la que va por las calles dentro del círculo de guardias como
    animal de cacería
es en verdad la única princesa de esta tierra.

Véanla ahora
subiendo los escalones de palacio: si desatadas van
las correas de sus sandalias, muy entradas en sus carnes
están las amarras de sus sagradas muñecas.

Gentes de Tebas,
ya Antígona y Creonte están en sus inevitables papeles.
Ella ocupa su asiento de reo
y él ahora no sólo es rey, sino la estentórea voz del destino
y su inclemencia.

CREONTE

Naciste
del vientre de mi hermana y lazo de amor te une a Hemón, mi
    hijo.
Eres, pues, más pariente mío que muchos.

Doble dolor y doble cólera arden en mi alma.
Es justo, entonces, que doble rigor tenga contigo.

Mi hijo Hemón deambula incrédulo por pasajes y
    habitaciones,
ya sabiéndose novio de una segura condenada.
Porque condenada estás desde que los bandos pregonaron la
    orden y el castigo.

Y sin embargo ríes, y esta insolencia es mayor que la del
    enterramiento
porque allí burlaste a simples y oscuros guardias
y aquí tu sorna y jactancia
son ante tu rey.

Siempre es más fácil ordenar la muerte
de aquel que comete un delito y luego lo toma a honra. Tu risa
hará que condenar también sea un placer.

XI

NARRADORA

People of Thebes,
who peep and hide like curious monkeys,
the one who walks the streets surrounded by sentinels
    like a preyed-upon beast,
is the only true princess of this land.

Look at her now
stepping up the stairs of the palace: though the straps
of her sandals are loosened, the bonds dig hard
into the flesh of her sacred wrists.

People of Thebes,
already Antígona and Creonte play their inescapable roles.
She takes the seat of the prisoner
and he is now not only king, but the stentorian voice of fate
and its severity.

CREONTE

Born
from my sister's womb, joined by love with Hemón,
    my son,
you are, I suppose, closer to me than many.

Double is the pain and anger that burn in my soul.
It is just, then, that I apply to you a doubled rigor.

My son Hemón wanders through corridors
    and halls,
in shock, knowing himself the groom
of a sure convict.
Because you've been condemned from the moment the order
    and the punishment were announced.

And you laugh all the same, and such insolence is worse
    than the act of burial,
for then you mocked simple and dull sentinels
but here all your scorn and arrogance
are in the face of your king.

It is always easier to punish with death
whomever commits a crime and then takes prides in himself.
    Your laughter
will make the punishment even pleasant.

¿Pero quién más ríe contigo?
¿Qué cómplices se ocultan en sus casas a gozar tu osadía?
¿Ismene, tu hermana, también te asistió y es la otra cabeza
de la víbora bicéfala?

ANTÍGONA

La víbora tiene una sola cabeza, Creonte.
Mi hermana Ismene es inocente. Sus pensamientos más
　　atrevidos
no van más allá de su tímido frontal.

Dices que he violado tu ley.
¿Pretendes tú, mortal, prevalecer
por encima de las leyes no escritas pero inquebrantables de
　　los dioses?

Sólo ellos tienen mandato sobre los cuerpos de los muertos.
Recuérdalo: sólo ellos.

Sé bien ·
que Polinices venía a devastar nuestra patria y que Etéocles la
　　defendía,
pero ahora, muertos, el Hades les otorga igualdad de derechos.

Como ves,
he preferido cumplir con los dioses y no con tu arrogante
　　capricho.

Sucumbir por tal motivo es ganancia, y no me duele.
Doleríame, sí, que el hijo de mi misma madre
quedara insepulto. Tú sigue llamándolo enemigo
hasta el fin de tus días,
pero yo he nacido para amar, no para compartir odios.

Ha de parecerte que hay sonido de locura en mis palabras,
pero no, la locura está en tus oídos.
¿Sabes que hay muchos tebanos que alzarían estas mismas
　　palabras,
que las dirían a voces por calles y plazas
si el miedo no les cerrara la boca?

Los dioses quieran, Creonte,
que no te dure el privilegio de ordenar impunemente lo que
　　te place,
y quieran también acabar pronto con tu gozo de escuchar
sólo el multitudinario
e indigno
silencio.

But who else laughs with you?
Who are the partners in crime hiding at home, rejoicing with your
    boldness?
Did your sister, Ismene, help you and is she the other head
of the bicephalous snake?

ANTÍGONA

The snake has only one head, Creonte.
My sister Ismene is blameless. Her boldest thoughts
do not go past her shy gaze.

You say I broke your law.
Do you, a mortal, expect to prevail
over the unwritten but unbreakable laws
    of the gods?

They alone hold power over the bodies of the dead.
Remember it: they alone.

I know it well,
Polinices came to ravage our country and Etéocles defended it.
But now, dead, Hades grants them equal rights.

As you see,
I've preferred to obey the gods, not your arrogant
    whim.

To die for such a cause is profit, and it does not hurt me.
That my own mother's son remained unburied
would hurt me. Keep calling him an enemy
until your last day,
but I was born to love, not to share hatred.

Perhaps you think there's a mad ring to my words,
but no, the tune is in your ears.
Do you know that many Thebans would raise these same
    words,
would cry them aloud through streets and squares,
if fear were not shutting their mouths?

May the gods will, Creonte,
that the privilege to dispense orders with impunity as it
    pleases you
does not last long,
and may they bring a prompt end to the pleasure you take in hearing
only the multitudinous,
indignant
silence.

XII

NARRADORA

No supongamos tanta dureza en el corazón del rey.
Seguramente ha vencido mil dudas antes de sancionar a la
    joven
que hizo promesa de amor con su hijo
y es tan cercana de su sangre.

Ay Antígona, qué hermosa y altiva presa eres. La escolta de
    guardias
no perturba tu caminar lento
y regio.

Vas mirando sin ansia
rostros en las ventanas, árboles, veredas, un brillo de sol
en una aldaba, y mil cosas que para ti son últimas.

No te llevan a cadalso, a final que viene raudo como viaje
de flecha o vuelo de hacha, no:
Creonte te ha señalado muerte para la memoria de todos,
    muerte
que se vocee así:
si tamaño castigo da a pariente ¿qué pueden esperar otros
    enemigos?
Vas, Antígona, a muerte más larga y perversa.

Entre el roquerío de la montaña
hay profundas y caprichosas cuevas. En una de ellas serás
    lanzada
y vastamente tapiada.
Cárcel te será
mientras te duren las interminables horas de hambre y sed y
    oscuridad
y luego secreta e inmensa tumba, porque no sólo te albergará
    la cueva
sino toda la montaña.

XII

NARRADORA

We should not assume too much harshness in the heart of the king.
Surely he defeated countless doubts before sanctioning
    the young woman,
who vowed love to his son
and is so near of blood.

Antígona, what a beautiful and arrogant prey you are! The escort
    of sentinels
does not trouble your steady and magnificent
gait.

You look without longing
at faces in the windows, trees, lanes, the glister of the sun
in a latch, and a thousand other things that for you are final.

They don't take you to the gallows, to an end that comes swift like
    the flight
of an arrow or the blow of an axe, no:
Creonte has appointed a death for the memory of all,
    a death
they will voice like this:
if he punishes his kin thus, what should other foes
    expect?
You go, Antígona, to a death longer and more perverse.

Amid the rocks in the mountain
there are deep, capricious caves. Into one of them you'll be
    cast
and shut in with wide boards.
It will be your prison
while endless hours prolong your hunger and thirst and
    darkness,
then it will be a secret and immense tomb, for not only the cave will
    harbour
    you,
but the entire mountain.

XIII

ANTÍGONA

La oscuridad le da a mi cuerpo una existencia extraña.
Soy
sólo cuando me palpo o toco la dura piedra de la caverna.
Cuando hablo no sé si hablo, acaso sólo sean palabras que
    circulan
sin sonido dentro de mi cabeza.

Esto
y la muerte
debo pagar en este tiempo de perversas confusiones.
La piedad, que antiguamente era virtud, hoy me condena
y alarga las desgracias de mi familia.

Los viejos dicen que un antiguo conjuro pesó sobre mi padre y
    mi madre
y que las desventuras, como las olas de la mar, se repetirán
de una generación a otra.
Y entonces desde aquí, aunque no me escuchen, viejos, yo les
    recuerdo
una ley del Olimpo
que dice
que nada grande entra en la vida de los hombres
sin alguna maldición.
Si la paz es esa cosa grande, yo soy la maldición, la ola rara
que se estrella y muere en el interior de esta cueva.

Lo siento por ti, amado Hemón. Éramos una mujer y un
    hombre soñando
ritos nupciales, banquetes y tálamos.
Otro será mi novio ahora, vendrá desde la oscuridad,
y comeré mi manjar, este aire,
y me tenderé sobre esta piedra que ese último día me parecerá
    de plumas.

XIII

ANTÍGONA

Darkness splits my body from its reality.
I am
only when I feel my skin or touch the rough stone of the cavern.

I don't know if I speak when I speak, perhaps these words
    only hover
mute inside my head.

This
and death
I should pay in these times of twisted turmoils.
Piety, which of old was virtue, now condemns me
and extends the woes of my family.

The old men say that an ancient curse weighed down upon my father
    and mother,
and that misfortunes, like the waves of the sea, will continue to break
from one generation to the next.
So, from here, though you can't hear me, old men, I
    remind you
of a law from Olympus
which says
that nothing great sets foot in the life of men
without a curse.
If peace is that great thing, I am the curse, the wayward wave
that breaks and dies from inside this cavern.

I'm sorry for you, my beloved Hemón. We were a woman and a
    man dreaming
of bridal ceremonies, of banquets, and bed.
Someone else will be my groom now, he will come from darkness,
and I will feast on this air,
and I will sleep on this stone, which will seem to me of feathers
on that last day.

XIV

NARRADORA

Desde la madrugada,
Hemón camina porque camina, va y viene
a ninguna parte
y sólo se detiene a mirar la montaña donde se consume
Antígona.

¿Qué ha sucedido en mi patria
para que ojos tan jóvenes miren con tanta amargura?

Anoche Hemón tuvo un sueño insensato:
Se vio repentinamente muerto
por una dorada flecha disparada por algún dios
        compadecido,
y así atravesado y finado
entró en sueños en la cueva para buscar entre las sombras
la amada sombra de su prometida.

La luz del alba le advirtió que soñaba, y odió la luz.
Se puso de pie y empezó a caminar al garete: igual
le era pisar yerba, piedra o grava.

Una pregunta le maduró en su deambular:
¿hasta dónde debe ir el amor por un padre? ¿Debemos pagar
esa deuda de origen
aun con la aceptación silenciosa de sus injusticias?

Hemón sabe que es pregunta rebelde, pero la lleva en el gesto
mientras sube a hablar con Creonte.

CREONTE

Hijo mío, oí rumor de tu despecho por tu frustrada boda,
pero mírame soy rey y padre, pero no dos personas, no uno
inflexible
y otro blando.
Mi firmeza de casa debe prolongarse a todos los rincones de
        la patria
donde debo ser obedecido en lo pequeño y en lo justo,
y aun en lo que no lo es.

XIV

NARRADORA

Since the crack of dawn
Hemón drifts back and forth,
going nowhere,
stopping only to look at the mountain where Antígona
    slowly burns.

What has happened in my country
that eyes so young look with so much sorrow?

Last night Hemón had an imprudent dream:
he saw himself dead in a trice
by a golden arrow fired from a sympathetic
    god,
and thus pierced and finished
he entered in dreams the cave, looking among the shadows
for the betrothed shadow of his lover.

Dawn's light told him he was dreaming, and he hated the light.
He stood up and walked adrift—all the same
to tread on grass, stone, or gravel.

A question ripened as he wandered:
How far should the love for a father go? Should we pay
that debt of birth
even with the silent acceptance of injustices?

Hemón knows it's a rebellious question, but he carries it
in his gait as he walks up to Creonte.

CREONTE

Son, I heard it rumored that you resent your arrested wedding,
but look at me: I am king and father, but not two persons, not one
    unyielding
and another lenient.
My domestic assertiveness must be prolonged to all corners
    of the fatherland,
where I must be obeyed in all matters, small and just,
and even in those that are not.

Engendrar hijos es un riesgo, Hemón.
Los que salen cortos de alma
sólo sirven para burla de los enemigos,
pero yo estoy confiado contigo, te di sentimientos fuertes
y sé que no podrán disolverse ante la apetencia
por el placer de una mujer.

Sepas, además, que sería sospechoso si no gélido
el abrazo desnudo de aquella que se ha portado enemiga
de nuestra estirpe.
Deja que ella encuentre un novio en el Hades
y tú, hijo mío, busca entre otras doncellas
otros campos donde labrar.

HEMÓN

Muy extraño es ser hijo de un poderoso.
Te escucho decir palabras domésticas de padre
juntamente con órdenes y leyes de rey.

Y privilegio siento en no verte
como el alto gobernante que a otros intimida.

Te pido permiso para usar ese privilegio,
y decirte lo que escucho en las calles, entre las sombras:
toda la ciudad llora a Antígona.
Los sencillos ciudadanos censuran la afrentosa muerte
que le estás dando. Dicen:
"aquella que no consintió que su hermano fuera pasto de
        perros,
¿no es acaso más digna de alcanzar honra que castigo?"

Óyelos, padre.

Yo quisiera para ti toda la sabiduría del mundo, pero los
        dioses
todavía no han creado a tal hombre.
No imites a los soberbios de mil talentos que cuando se les
                casca
son hueros.

To procreate is a risk, Hemón.
Children with small spirits
are only objects of laughter for the enemy,
but I am confident in you, I've passed on to you my robust feelings
and I know the appetite of female pleasure
couldn't wither them.

Know, also, that her naked embrace would be suspicious
if not frigid,
behaving as she did like an enemy to our race.
Let her find a groom in Hades,
and you, my son, look to other maidens
other fertile fields.

HEMÓN

Being the son of a strongman is very strange.
I hear you saying the domestic words of a father
together with the orders and laws of a king.

And I take it as a privilege not seeing you
like the high ruler who intimidates others.

I ask your permission to use this privilege,
and tell you what I hear on the streets, among the shadows:
the entire city cries for Antígona.
The modest citizens condemn the outrageous death
you are giving her. They say:
"Isn't she who wouldn't stand for her brother being left to the dogs
more worthy of praise than punishment?"

Listen to them, father.

I should want for you a perfect wisdom, but the
       gods
have not yet created such a man.
Don't copy the hubristic man of the ten thousand talents
       who when cracked
was vacuous.

Oye a los sencillos ciudadanos, padre.

Que no te sea humillante el aprender de ellos.
Que tus leyes no sean de tu solo arbitrio, porque no es patria
lo que es posesión de un solo hombre.

También oye a los dioses. Mira la noche
porque en el silencio estelar,
ellos piden que no olvides ni pisotees sus derechos sobre los
    muertos.

Oye a todos, padre, y cede,
y revoca la dura orden para que todos celebremos la paz
y Antígona la luz.

Listen to the modest citizens, father.

Let not learning from them be a humiliation.
Don't make laws from your sole judgement, because a fatherland
cannot belong to a single man alone.

Listen to the gods as well. Look at the night,
—in the starry silence
they are asking you not to forget or thrash their rights upon
　　　the dead.

Listen to them all, father, and yield,
and revoke the cruel order, so that we can all celebrate peace
and Antígona the light.

XV

NARRADORA

Las vivaces cabras saltan de peña en peña
y se aparean
sin sospechar que en el vientre de la soleada montaña
hay una cueva
que es cárcel perpetua y tumba y tálamo.

Hasta allí no penetra el sagrado ojo del día
ni el llanto de amigos y parientes. En ese silencio
la muerte laboriosa envuelve a la joven condenada
en un denso capullo de sombras.

ANTÍGONA

Yo quise ser la justa enterradora
y ser enterrada es el premio que he recogido.

Padre mío,
madre mía,
hermanos Etéocles y Polinices, ya siento que toco las manos
    de ustedes
que las alargan hacia mí desde el otro mundo.

Moriré sin cantos de himeneo
ni caricias de esposo
ni crianza de un niño. Sólo he llegado a ser hija y hermana
    grata,
recíbanme como tal.

Curiosa es mi muerte. Mi cuerpo joven
no tiene destructora ni cruel enfermedad,
y aquí no espero el imposible golpe de una espada ciega
para que yo muera regando mi sangre.
Me estoy acabando lentamente: en la misma medida que
    consumo la vida
entra en mí
y crece
el dulce abandono que llamamos muerte.

XV

NARRADORA

The lively goats frolic on the rocks
and mate,
unmindful that the cave inside the womb
of the sunlit mountain
is a perpetual prison, and tomb, and a marriage bed.

The sacred eye of daylight does not penetrate that far
nor do the cries of friends and relatives. In that silence,
death, laborious, enfolds the girl
in a dense cocoon of shadows.

ANTÍGONA

I wanted to be the just gravedigger
but a grave for myself is the prize I've received.

Dear father,
dear mother,
        brothers, Etéocles and Polinices, I already feel the touch of your
                hands,
you stretch them out to me from the other world.

I will die without Hymeneal songs
or the touch of a husband,
never raising children. I've been but a daughter and a pleasing
        sister,
receive me as such.

Mine is a curious death. My young body
does not suffer a fatal or cruel disease
nor do I await the impossible blow of a blind sword
to kill me spilling my blood.
I waste away slowly: at the same time
        I consume my life,
it enters me
and grows
the sweet abandonment we call death.

XVI

NARRADORA

Un extranjero que cruzara Tebas de paso
vería un pueblo de orden, un rey que gobierna
y un pueblo que labora calmo.
No vería las turbulencias debajo del agua mansa.
¿Quién le diría
que una muchacha está muriendo por piadosa?

¿Quién le informaría
de que el joven iracundo que sale de palacio se arrancaría la piel
si con ello dejara de ser hijo del rey?

Y ahora sospechemos que serán más duras las secretas
    correntadas
porque ahí viene Tiresias, el anciano vidente: mala señal
es su caminar agobiado, que no es por edad sino por el peso
de sus presagios.

Los dioses le dieron a Tiresias una paradoja:
lo cegaron para que viera más lejos,
y así va, confiando sus pasos a un lazarillo, ante Creonte.

TIRESIAS

Tú puedes jurar, rey, que tu trono está sobre amplias bases de
    mármol.
Yo lo veo al borde de un abismo.

Escúchame:
Están ocurriendo sucesos para el temor.
Los mil pájaros de mi árbol, pájaros de algarabía,
fueren expulsados por grandes aves llenas de cólera
que hicieron del árbol campo de batalla
done esgrimían garras para sangrarse cruelmente.

XVI

NARRADORA

A stranger who passed by Thebes
would see a town in order, a king ruling
and a people working calmly.
He would not see the turbulence under the still water.

Who would tell him
that a young woman dies for her piety?

Who would inform him
that the young man who leaves the palace full of anger would peel
off his skin,
if he could thus cease being the son of the king?

And now we must suspect the secret
        torrents
will be worse, for here comes Tiresias, the old seer: a bad sign
is his heavy walking, not with age but the weight
of his prophecies.

The gods gifted Tiresias with a paradox:
they made him blind so that he could see farther,
and thus he goes, entrusting his steps to a guide, towards Creonte.

TIRESIAS

You could swear, king, that your throne stands on a vast pedestal
        of marble.
I see it on a razor's edge.

Listen:
Things are happening that point to fear.
The thousand birds on my tree, joyful birds,
were driven off by large raptors full of anger
who turned the tree into a battleground
where they brandished their claws to cruelly bleed one another.

Al no comprender esa violencia, acaso
figuración de otra venidera,
yo corrí a ofrecer sacrificios en el altar. Puse sobre el hornillo
las ofrendas habituales, frescos húmeros de oveja y buey, y
    pequeñas vejigas
de hiel,
y todo untado con grasa para avivar el fuego,
pero, ay, el fuego no levantó sus lenguas,
y la grasa se derritió gota a gota sobre el rescoldo dando gran
    humo, y la hiel
salpicó el aire oscuro y atosigante.

Dime, Creonte ¿por qué los dioses rechazaron mi sacrificio?

Y asimismo es en todos los altares, y es casa por casa
como una peste. Y aves y perros llegan a los hornillos
como siguiendo una orden
y los atestan con piltrafas arrancadas del cadáver de Polinices.
¿Acaso es necesario mi arte de vidente para interpretar tales
    signos?

Tú retaste a los dioses, pero todo Tebas paga tu insolencia.

Me retiro pidiéndote que no punces más al cadáver.
    Entiérralo.
Que se diga que fuiste valiente corrigiendo tu yerro
y no valiente volviendo a matar al que está ya matado.

As I couldn't understand such violence, perhaps
an omen of another a future one,
I rushed to offer sacrifices on the altar. I placed the customary
offerings
on the fire, fresh humerus of sheep and ox and
small gallbladders,
everything anointed with fat as to fuel the fire,
but, oh, the fire did not raise its tongues
and the melted fat dripped over the ember, making a great smoke,
and the bile
spattered the dark and poisonous air.

Tell me, Creonte, why did the gods reject my sacrifice?

And it is the same on all the altars, house by house
like a plague. Birds and dogs approach the fires,
as if they were following orders,
and pack them with scraps from Polinices' corpse.
Is my art of prophecy really necessary to interpret such
signs?

You defied the gods, but all Thebes pays for your insolence.

I take my leave asking you to stop pricking the corpse.
    Bury it.
Let it be said you had the courage to rectify your mistake,
not that you were brave to kill a man already dead.

XVII

NARRADORA

Nadie alrededor. Creonte está sentado solo en el centro del
    gran salón.
Se mira en el espejo
y ve un hombre irritado tomando vino.
Y nadie alrededor.

El vino es de las cepas reales,
pero sus pensamientos caen en el vaso y la bebida se tuerce.

Y nadie alrededor.

CREONTE

¿Quién no está contra mí?
¿Hemón, mi hijo subyugado por una vil mujer?
¿Tiresias, el viejo adivino, que me culpa de las llamas muertas
    en los altares
sin ver la hartura de los dioses que ya no desean las ofrendas
de los pusilánimes?
¿Quién no está disparando flechas contra mí?
¿Quién no me trajinaría como mercancía si hubiera
    comprador?

Pero una vez más digo: a Polinices
no lo enterrarán nunca en un sepulcro
aunque las águilas
le arranquen piltrafas y las lleven hasta el mismo trono de
    Zeus.

XVII

NARRADORA

No one around. Creonte sits alone in the center
 of the great hall.
He looks at himself in the mirror
and sees a vexed man drinking wine.

And no one around.

The wine comes from the royal vines,
but his thoughts fall into the glass and distort the drink.

And no one around.

CREONTE

Who is not against me?
Hemón? My son, under the yoke of a vile woman?
Tiresias? The old seer, who blames me for the dead
 flames in the altars,
unaware that the gods, fully sated, don't want offerings
 from cowards?
Who's not shooting arrows at me?
Who wouldn't trade me as merchandise, were there a buyer?

But I'll say it once again: No one
will bury Polinices under the earth,
not even if the eagles
tear apart his corpse and carry the scraps all the way up to the very
 throne of Zeus.

XVIII

NARRADORA

Tiresias, el anciano de los ojos muertos,
convierte todo su cuerpo en un enorme ojo, no para ver lo de
hoy
sino lo de mañana.

Anoche no pudo entrar en el sueño
y estuvo mirando calamidades
que el tiempo está trayendo rápidamente hacia Tebas.

Apenas sintió el sol del amanecer en su vieja piel
puso la mano sobre el hombro del lazarillo
y enrumbó por el camino de palacio. Lleva premoniciones,
hechos espantables
que ya no puede contener en su boca.

TIRESIAS

Otra vez he venido hasta ti, Creonte, para pedirte que hagas
humilde silencio
escuches cómo vienen
las Furias del Hades
y de los dioses. Se acercan
veloces y vengadoras, y tú eres la presa ineludible.

Tú, porque crees que tu crecido poder alcanza para gobernar
otros mundos.
Tienes retenido a Polinices en el mundo de abajo,
perteneciendo,
como todos los muertos, al mundo de arriba.
Y en un juego contrario,
tienes en una cueva, que es tumba de muerto,
a Antígona, que aunque desfalleciente, aún es viva.

Anoche me llegaron imágenes de tu desastre. Quise alejarlas
bañando mi frente con agua fresca, pero volvían
una y otra vez. Vi
la terrible cobranza de los dioses: entre todos se llevaban
un ser surgido de tu propio ser, el más querido.
Y aun ahora que hablo contigo
me viene un largo olor de sangre, un olor adelantado, tal vez
de mañana.

XVIII

NARRADORA

Tiresias, the old man with dead eyes,
turns his whole body into an enormous eye,
to see not the things
    of today
but tomorrow's.

Last night he could not enter into sleep
only seeing the calamities
that time hastens to Thebes.

As soon as he felt the morning sun on his old skin
he placed his hand on the guide's shoulder
and set off onto the royal road. He carries premonitions,
awful deeds
he can't keep shut in his mouth any longer.

TIRESIAS

I've come to you once more, Creonte, to ask for
    your humble silence,
that you listen to them coming,
the Furies from Hades
and from the gods. They're closing in,
swift and vengeful, and you are the inescapable prey.

You, believing your swollen power enough to rule
    in other realms,
retain Polinices in the world below,
    when he belongs
like all dead, to the world above.
And playing the opposite game,
you keep Antígona in a cavern that is a dead person's tomb,
while she, though fainting, is still alive.

Last night, I received visions of your downfall. I tried
driving them away, moistening my forehead with fresh water,
but they came back, over and over. I saw
the terrible requital of the gods: of all men, they took
one born from your own being, the dearest.
Even now as I speak,
I can smell a long scent of blood, coming ahead of time, maybe from
    tomorrow.

Evita, Creonte, el vuelo de las Furias, haz que desistan
de su desquite
y regresen a sus mundos. Deja tu ceguera
que es peor que la mía, porque no es de ojos de carne sino de
    soberbia
y escúchame:

ya sabes que el consejo es mayor cuando aparta el peor de
    los males,
y este que te dejo es de los mayores: entierra al muerto
y libera a su fiel hermana, y prontamente
porque cada hora
la sangre que viene hacia ti huele más próxima.

Prevent, Creonte, the coming flight of the Furies, make them cease
their retaliation
and go back to their worlds. Let go of your blindness
—it's worse than mine, not of flesh but
    of arrogance—
and listen:

you know advice is greater when it averts the worst
    of evils
and this counsel I'm lending you is among the greatest: bury the dead
    man
and free his faithful sister, promptly,
for every hour
the blood coming to you smells closer.

XIX

NARRADORA

No hay peor tortura que la propia imaginación
y Antígona no cesa en mi mente.

La veo esperando que se forme una imposible gota de agua
en la piedra árida
y caiga en su boca sedienta,
o tanteando en ese mundo inhóspito una yerba amarga
para su infinita hambre,
o pronunciando lentas palabras para que su propia voz la
    acompañe
mientras entra en el letargo
doblándose sobre sí misma como una figurilla de cera.

ANTÍGONA

(Habla como lejana y jugando con una cinta de seda que ha desatado de su
    cintura, la enrolla y desenrolla en su brazo)

Soñé que amanecía. Qué absurdo,
soñé que amanecía.

Tal vez el amanecer esté encima de la montaña,
pero no tendrá la luz esplendente de mi sueño.

La luz que vi era otra
y yo quería entrar en ella y disolverme en su liviandad.

Ay si ese fuera el camino para entrar en el Hades, y ser luz
repentina, cuerpo huido de este suplicio
largo y perverso.

Ay si pudiera tomar ese camino, esa puerta rápida, ese atajo.

XIX

NARRADORA

There's no worse torture than one's own imagination
and Antígona does not fade in my mind.

I see her waiting for an impossible drop of water to form
on the arid rock
and fall in her thirsty mouth,
or groping in that forbidding world for a bitter green
for her infinite hunger,
or muttering slow words, so that her own voice
    accompanies her,
while her body falls into a lethargy
folding forward like a wax figurine.

ANTÍGONA

*(She speaks absent-mindedly and plays with a silk ribbon she's loosened from
    her waist, twisting and untwisting it around her arm)*

I dreamed of dawn. How absurd,
I dreamed of dawn.

Perhaps dawn's light falls on top of the mountain,
though it wouldn't have the luminous quality of my dream.

The light I saw was different,
I wanted to enter it and dissolve in its nimble quality.

Oh, if only that were the road to step into Hades, and I
were a sudden light, a body withdrawn from this torture
long and perverse.

Oh, if only I could take that road, that quick gate, that
    short path.

XX

NARRADORA

Desde temprano
los clarines reales han llamado a la población a las puertas de
    palacio,
pero los tebanos, antes sólo gente de acatamiento, hoy
han traído algo para enrostrar. Gritarán
que sus altares siguen inservibles, ahogados como están los
    fuegos
por las piltrafas de Polinices.

Pero Creonte los ha sorprendido. Ha salido al atrio
con otro rostro. Nadie sabe si por la razón o el miedo,
pero comparable está a un pescador que ha desatado cien
    nudos
toda la noche
y a la mañana siguiente ve satisfecho y en paz su cuerda lisa.

Cien nudos toda la noche, y nadie sabe si desatados
por la razón o el miedo.

CREONTE

Pueblo de Tebas:
dar una orden y luego suspenderla no debe ser costumbre de
    gobierno,
pero si la dicha orden trae zozobra
y la insistencia en ella
puede estrellar al pueblo y a mí mismo contra la fatalidad,
es hora de revocarla.

Ustedes esperaban íntimamente esta decisión. Que sus
    corazones entonces
se alegren este día
porque doy licencia para que vayan a hacerle entierro al muerto.
Llévenle
entre cantos
su derecho a ser cobijado por esta su tierra nativa.

XX

NARRADORA

From early morning
the royal trumpets have called the people to the gates
      of the palace,
but the Thebans, who were once all-obeying, today
have come carrying reproach. They will cry out
that their altars remain useless, the fires
      quenched
by Polinices' scraps.

But Creonte has surprised them. He came out to the atrium
with a different countenance. No one knows if moved by reason or
fear,
but he's like a fisherman who loosened a hundred
      knots
all night,
and the next morning, satisfied and peaceful, looks at his
smooth rope.

A hundred knots all night, and no one knows if loosened
by reason or fear.

CREONTE

People of Thebes:
to give an order and then take it back must not be a habit
      of government,
but if such an order produces sorrow
and if insisting upon it
can thrust the people and myself into fatality,
it is time to revoke it.

You were privately waiting for this decision. Let
      your hearts then
be gladdened on this day,
because I am giving you permission to go and bury
      the dead man.
Bring him
amid songs
his right to be sheltered by this, his native land.

Yo voy a hacer el gesto contrario. Marcho a la montaña
a destruir el sello de piedras
que enclaustra a Antígona y la aleja
de la luz
y del amor de mi hijo Hemón, que hace días me sesga su
mirada.

Vayamos pronto,
y que los dioses se complazcan viéndonos trabajar en ello.

I will make the opposite gesture. I am setting off to the mountain
to break the seal of stone
cloistering Antígona and keeping her far
from light
and from my son Hemón's love, who for days now
        has looked at me sideways.

Let us go soon
and may the gods be pleased seeing us at work.

XXI

NARRADORA

El sello de piedras estaba roto
y el recién llegado Creonte miró el forado incrédulo y
    ofendido,
y abrevió
para los cielos y la tierra
toda su rabia en una pregunta: "¿quién el atrevido?", gritó.

Por el forado, más hechura de zarpas desesperadas que de
    manos humanas,
entraron guardias con antorchas y el rey con su cólera.

Y avanzando hacia el fondo oscuro
vino hacia ellos un sobrecogedor lamento. Era la voz
de Hemón,
pero Creonte la negó diciendo que era cruel burla de los
    dioses.

¿También quisiste negar, rey, la imagen que las antorchas
iluminaron?

Antígona colgando de su fino cuello, enlazada
por una cinta de seda roja a la saliente de una roca,
Hemón abrazando su cadáver por la cintura, llorando
su demorado atrevimiento para romper el sello.

Cuando el joven sintió la luz, volteó el rostro y más fuego
que en las antorchas había en sus ojos.

El rencor produce una saliva ácida, y con ella
ensució la cara de su padre
antes de atacarlo con el doble filo de su espada. El hijo
sólo hirió el aire, el sitio vacío
que había dejado el esquivado y ágil cuerpo de Creonte.

Burlado en su ataque, Hemón levantó la espada
y se la hundió a sí mismo en la mitad del pecho. Feroz signo
de ira contra su propio padre.

La vida sólo estuvo con él el tiempo que necesitó para girar,
abrazar a Antígona,
y mojar las mejillas pálidas de su novia con la sangre que le
    subía a la boca.

Oh dioses, en las paredes de la cueva, sus sombras
eran las de dos jóvenes ceñidos
como en día de boda.

NARRADORA

The stone seal was broken
and, as he arrived, Creonte looked at the opening in the wall,
      incredulous and
      offended,
and condensed
for the skies and the earth
all his anger into one question: "Who? Who dares?," he screamed.

Through the opening, more the making of desperate claws than of
      human hands,
guards went in with torches and the king with his anger.

As they advanced to the dark depths
a dreadful moan reached them. It was the voice
of Hemón
but Creonte denied it, saying it was a cruel joke from
      the gods.
Did you also wish to deny, king, the image the torches
      illuminated?

Antígona hanging from her fine neck, fastened
by a red silk ribbon to the ledge of a rock,
Hemón embracing her corpse by the waist, lamenting
his late daring to break the seal.

When the boy felt the light, he turned his face and more fire
burned in his eyes than in the torches.

Bitterness produces an acidic spit, with this
he splattered the face of his father
before attacking him with the double edge of his sword. The son
only wounded the air, the empty space
left by Creonte's agile and swerving body.

His attack outsmarted, Hemón raised up his sword
and thrust it into his own chest. A fierce sign
of wrath against his own father.

Life was with him only enough to turn around,
embrace Antígona
and wet the pale cheeks of his lover with the blood coming
      up to his mouth.

Oh gods, in the walls of the cave, their shadows
were of two young lovers, closely fitted
as on a wedding day.

XXII

NARRADORA

Las muertes de esta historia vienen a mí
no para que haga oficio de contar desgracias ajenas.
Vienen a mí, y tan vivamente, porque son mi propia
    desgracia:
yo soy la hermana que fue maniatada por el miedo.

Antígona entró en mi casa como un airado y súbito fulgor
y me habló así: "Ismene,
quiero que tus manos me ayuden a sepultar el cadáver de
    nuestro amado hermano,
confío
en que habiendo nacido noble
no te haya ganado la villanía".

Sus palabras ardían,
pero yo tenía el ánimo como el de un pequeño animal
encogido,
y sabiendo que le asistía razón,
le dije que deliraba, que un aire de locura le había golpeado
    la cabeza.
Era el miedo, Antígona, porque la muerte sería nuestro pago
por enterrarle.
Ven, hermana, te rogué, mejor pidamos a los muertos que nos
    dispensen
y que prevalezcan sobre nosotras las órdenes de los poderosos
    vivos,
pero me reprochaste, dijiste "busca tú, Ismene,
la aprobación del mundo del tirano, yo iré tras la gracia
de los dioses", y te fuiste
a la colina de nuestro muerto.
(Abre un atado y descubre la mascarilla mortuoria de
Polinices. Entre las pausas de su parlamento le hace tres libaciones.)

XXII

NARRADORA

The deaths of this story come to me
not so that I make a trade of telling other people's misfortunes.
They come to me, and so vividly, because they are my own
    misfortune:
I am the sister who was hand-tied by fear.

Antígona came into my house like a furious sudden flash
and spoke to me: "Ismene,
I want your hands to help me bury the corpse of
    our beloved brother,
I trust
that, born noble,
you have not turned petty."

Her words were seething
but I had the spirit of a little animal,
huddled up,
and knowing that reason tended her
I said she was raving, that a blow of madness had struck
    her head.

It was fear, Antígona, because death would be our penalty
    for burying him.
Come, my sister, I begged you, let us rather ask the dead
    to excuse us
and let the orders of the living powers
    prevail,
but you rebuked me, saying: "You, Ismene, seek
assent from the world of the tyrant, I'll go after the favor
of the gods," and left
for the hill of our dead.
(She unwraps something and uncovers Polinices' mortuary mask.
After each stanza, she offers a libation.)

Antígona,
¿ves este mundo de abajo?
El palacio tiene ahora un profundo silencio de mausoleo
y desde ahí nos gobierna un cadáver que respira, un rey
atormentado
que velozmente se hace viejo.

Hermana mía, mira:
este es el rostro de nuestro hermano antes de los perros
y los buitres y la podredumbre,
y estas libaciones tardías son de mi pequeña alma culposa.

En tu elevado reino
pídele a Polinices que me perdone la tarea que no hice a
tiempo
porque me acobardó el caño del poder, y dile
que ya tengo castigo grande:
el recordar cada día tu gesto
que me tortura
y me avergüenza.

(Telón)

Antígona,
do you see this world below?
The palace now bears the silence of a mausoleum
and from there we are ruled by a breathing corpse, a king,
tormented,
who grows old swiftly.

Dear sister, look:
this is the face of our brother as it was before the dogs
and the vultures and putrefaction,
and these late libations are from my little spirit full of remorse.

In your elevated kingdom
ask Polinices to forgive me for the duty I did not do at the right time
because I shrank in the furrowed face of power, and tell him
that I already have a heavy punishment:
to remember, every day, your deed,
which tortures
and brings me to shame.

(Curtain)

3
ANGLES OF MEMORY IN *ANTÍGONA*
An aesthetic reading

An aesthetic approach

Antígona, as mentioned in the Introduction, is both a performance and a literary text. There is no paradox here: this text is meant *both* to be performed *and* to be read.[1] The study of either the performance or the text requires different methodologies, and *Antígona* (or any text, for that matter) operates differently in each of these two aspects. Furthermore, the two different approaches yield different insights, which makes the text, in turn, the richer. This is already true if we were studying *Antígona* in Spanish, for, as we also saw in the Introduction, the poetics of the original performer and those of the written text do not completely coincide, the performance being inscribed onto the actress' experience in Peru, while the written text remains purposefully uninscribed. Yet the event of translation removes even more the attachment of the text to its original context of emergence and performance, as it changes the context of reception, inviting even more proliferations and displacements of meaning. Thus, it becomes all the more important to think about the text as never fully determined by its original circumstances and to expand what we understand by "context." Charles Martindale (following Derrida) puts it nicely when he addresses reductive and positivistic historical readings thus: "one trouble with contexts is that there are too many of them. Contexts are not single, nor are they found 'lying about' as it were; we have to construct them from other texts, which also have to be interpreted" (*Redeeming the Text* 13). Sophocles' *Antigone* and "Antigone" as the larger body of interpretations of the myth constitute

DOI: 10.4324/9781003150350-3

texts from which *Antígona*'s "context" can and should be construed. My approach echoes a deconstructivist insistence that context is "never saturated" (Derrida "Signature Event Context" 310). Thus, I will think of "context" differently than exclusively historical or cultural.

My interest here is on textual aspects that have been disregarded in the scholarship, and because of that I will forego performative elements. I focus particularly on one of *Antígona*'s most important aspects—namely, that it "adapts" another text. I care about the particular pleasure we find in adaptation, following Linda Hutcheon's argument that such pleasure comes from "repetition and variation" and that "recognition and remembrance" are also part of it (*Adaptation* 4).[2] Yet my textual reading of *Antígona* also takes up Eve Kosofsky Sedgwick's invitation to a form of thinking that assemblages itself *beside*, comprising a wide range of relations like "desiring, identifying, representing, repelling, paralleling, differentiating, rivaling, leaning, twisting, mimicking, withdrawing, attracting, aggressing, warping" (*Touching Feeling* 8). Thus, "to adapt" here also means to desire, rival, twist, mimic, repel, etc. As I will explain in the next section, I look at these textual relations using memory as a heuristic metaphor, noting especially how gestures of remembering and forgetting position the text with respect to Sophocles' *Antigone* and "Antigone," and how they generate the spaces for its politics and affects, a positioning and a generation that are part of the pleasure of this text.[3]

The transformative relationship between two texts that Hutcheon calls "adaptation" has been termed "hypertextuality" by Gerard Genette. In *Palimpsests*, which remains one of the most important works on the theory of poetics—the study of the types of discourse, modes of enunciation, and literary genres "from which emerges each singular text" (1)—Genette defines hypertextuality as "any relationship uniting a text B … to an earlier text A … upon which it is grafted in a manner that is not that of commentary" (5). Following Genette's terminology, I will call Sophocles' *Antigone* the "hypotext" and Watanabe's the "hypertext." Genette's framework is enabling in as much as it renders visible literary operations key to *Antígona*'s ways of making meaning as well as (*beside*) its deployment of affects—that is, the operations key to the text's "emergence," to expand on Genette's word, or to the text's pleasure, to stay with Hutcheon (and Rolland Barthes).

I also build on Sedgwick's assessment that, after more than a century of dominant approaches to interpretation that privilege suspicion and the need for unveiling hidden structures of truth, we should find it helpful to take recourse to what she calls "weak" theories and "reparative" readings.[4]

My approach, putting Genette *beside* affect theory, is decidedly "weak" and "aesthetic"[5] and focused on close reading,[6] as if taking its prompt from Eugenie Brinkema's question: "What would happen to the study of both affectivity and form if we were to reintroduce close reading to the study of sensation?" (xvi). Yet my formal, weak, or "reparative" reading is still informed by other "strong" theoretical approaches, that is, critical frames that can "organize vast amounts of territory and tell big truths," as Heather Love succinctly puts Silvan Tomkins's definition of strong theories (Love 237). These are necessary to keep oneself and the reader alert to the fact that the encounter between two texts does not take place in a historical vacuum and is thus not only formal and textual (in a common sense understanding of a written text) but is an assemblage of encounters between cultures and, as such, always marked by (often asymmetrical) power dynamics between those cultures.[7] Without denying the reality of cultural and political hegemony, my reading is not an analysis of it (nor of its subversion)—a form of analysis which, as Sedgewick notes, can often be self-reinforcing of the hegemony it aims at dismantling (*Touching Feeling* 12). I look at the literary operations, textures, through which *Antígona* grafts itself into contextual assemblages where geographical and political borders do not exhaust its meanings and doings.

Someone might think that, in taking this "aesthetic" approach to my analysis of *Antígona* as a "version" of Sophocles' *Antigone*, I seem to be putting the weight on the hypertext's "dependent" character with respect to the Greek "model." Arguably, this vertical orientation of "influence" would also sustain a political hierarchy, in which the work of literature produced by a subaltern author (Watanabe and Ralli) is construed as less "original,"[8] hence less authoritative, than the one produced by an ancient Greek (Sophocles), perceived as a member of a hegemonic European culture.[9] And this would carry with it a proliferating chain of ideological prejudices and constructs, in which, for instance, Latin American literature is historically perceived as a superfluous repetition and imitation of the hierarchically "superior" (and "original") European culture.[10] My "aesthetic" approach could thus be subjected to a criticism like the one expressed by Moira Fradinger in her study of *Antigone*'s afterlife in Latin America. Fradinger argues that readings that take what she calls a "compare and contrast" approach produce a "mystification" of the model, as if it contained "universal themes and values," which, in her view, is "a fantasy that overlooks, on the one hand, the real impossibility of equating modern culture with that of ancient Athens, and on the other hand, the cultural transactions through which Europeans transformed the ancient tragedy

("Antígonas" 224). I agree with Fradinger that we cannot equate ancient and modern cultures and that there is nothing universal about Sophocles' *Antigone* (or any ancient Greek text, for that matter). However, I do not think that a hypertextual ("compare and contrast") reading necessarily equates the two disparate historical realities, for I am not establishing an analogy between cultures but rather signaling the interventions from one historical moment into another one. Nor is a hypertextual analysis necessarily at odds with an awareness of "the cultural transactions through which Europeans transformed the ancient tragedy." In fact, the gesture of transforming tragedy through hypertextual practices is already in itself a testament to the historicity and constructedness of a text and of its value. Thus, contrary to Fradinger's belief, the study of those gestures of transformation participates in the process of demystification of the source, as Lorna Hardwick has argued ("Greek Drama"). Most importantly, these different modes of reading (e.g. comparative cultural history and hypertextual analysis) are but different assemblages of the many contexts where readers can situate the text. I do not see why an assemblage that reads *Antígona* "regionally" in the context of other Latin American recreations should be privileged over other assemblages, unless one's purpose is to construe a cultural history of *Antígona* in Latin America, which is not my purpose here.

In a case like *Antígona*, there is no denying the relationship of imitation. For one, the title and subtitle—"Antígona: A Free Version of Sophocles' Tragedy"—openly announce that relationship. Our task is not denying that relationship but rather constructing a discourse capable of looking at it without sustaining an ideological hierarchy (Fradinger's "mystification")—which nostalgic and humanistic readings certainly sustain. Thus, Linda Hutcheon's argument that "an adaptation is a derivation that is not derivative—a work that is second without being secondary" (*Adaptation* 9) proves enabling for reading this text. It is a productive response to the moral and political issue of imitation, as it dismounts the presumed metaphysics implied in imitation when understood hierarchically and thus also avoids reinstating the cultural hegemony of the source text with respect to its successors. (Of course, postmodern theories, on which Hutcheon's work hinges, had already concerned themselves exhaustively with the ontological problem at the bottom of the concept of imitation: to reconceptualize difference and repetition, copy and original, in a non-hierarchical—Platonic, metaphysical—way.) Also following deconstructivist critiques of the idea of an "original" text, of which later versions would be a "copy," the concept of the "transhistorical" has been championed by classical reception scholars[11] as one that looks at the historical temporality of texts as a constant bi-directional movement that destabilizes both the past and the present, with the result that they can never be closed and identical with themselves. Although this concept is helpful to think of the ways in which modern readings always already shape the meaning of an ancient text, nonetheless the dialogical element in the notion of transhistoricity is lacking in some important ways, as Lorna Hardwick has suggested most recently ("Aspiration and Mantras"). For, while that concept destabilizes a presumed hierarchy between the "original" and the "copy," it does not necessarily help to address dynamics operating on a horizontal axis, that is, in the specific presents of both the ancient source and the modern version at each moment of reception. It is on that horizontal axis where asymmetrical power dynamics inflected by gender, race, ethnicity, and class are present at any given moment in time and constitute multiple contextual assemblages of the texts.[12] I have found that a reading guided by hypertextuality and aesthetics—understood in the broadest sense to include both formal aspects and feelings and affects—is good to think *beside* other readings that pay more attention to cultural referentiality and thus expand on the text's manifold capacities.

Memory as a metaphor

The theme of memory and forgetting makes its way into *Antígona* from the very first poem, as the Narradora celebrates that "today is the first day of the peace"[13] and invites readers and spectators to "start to forget" the war that has just ended. Yet in what follows, the play complicates the possibility of forgetting the war and the idea that it is over. As the Narradora herself takes on the task of narrating the events of the tragedy, it becomes clear that she is hardly able to follow her own injunction of oblivion. Rather, she becomes more and more invested in the opposite exercise, that of memorializing and remembering the events that ended in the deaths of Antígona and Hemón, and the fractures those deaths left in the society that witnessed them. Furthermore, when, in the last poem/scene, the Narradora finally reveals her identity as Ismene, "the sister who was hand-tied by fear," the entire text is retrospectively revealed to be an exercise of memory, of remembering. The surviving sister has not been able to forget; the insistence and persistence of memory has led her to brood over the events, narrating them to an audience so as to heal and forgive herself, as she confesses: "these late libations are from my little spirit full of remorse" (XXII).

Still, even if the Narradora has not been able to forget the war, memory always involves oblivion, a process of selection that is as much about what is remembered as it is about what is left out.[14] So perhaps the war and the deaths, the trauma, are not forgotten and must not be; but the story is not told completely. For the story of this war, the story of Antigone and her siblings does not start with this Narradora's rendition of it. It belongs to a much larger memory, to chains of tellings and retellings of this myth, to an "obstinate memory" (Fradinger, "Demanding the Political" 63) within which every instance of utterance ought to be situated.[15] What it remembers and what it forgets of those other retellings is essential to the text's "emergence," to quote Genette again. Hence, the guiding question in this chapter is precisely how this *Antígona* both remembers and forgets some important aspects of those chains of interpretations of the myth we call "Antigone"—though I focus mostly on Sophocles' *Antigone*, since Watanabe used it as a model and is explicitly oriented towards it (e.g. citing entire lines from it).

The title and subtitle's announcement of a hypertextual relationship to Sophocles' *Antigone* not only signals memory as an important operation *within* the text, but it has also two important consequences for the memory of readers. First, it places us in a (potential) situation of complicity with the Narradora, for we too are (potentially) in the know about the myth behind the story, we too might remember what is going to happen, how it all ends. At the same time, the subtitle also inscribes this text as a "free version," thus introducing difference within the repetition suggested by the title (*Antígona*). And this difference means that we do not necessarily remember the story *as* the Narradora remembers it; her memory is a new, unique memory of the myth, with its own instances of forgetting, which we are not in the know of (yet). But if we are in a position of complicity, that means that as we read we are also (potentially) able to recognize those differences, departures, elements that are missing, and things that are present but in a different way. While not every reader can be presumed to have read Sophocles' *Antigone* and to know the myth of which this text claims to be a version (*Antígona* is certainly enjoyable and comprehensible without that background), and while there are many ways of reading and different levels of engagement, the hypertextual component is one important way in which the text makes meaning and gives pleasure, once it is fleshed out.[16]

Hence, *Antígona* thematizes memory as one of its main concerns, mirrors that theme in its formal and hypertextual operations with respect to *Antigone* and "Antigone," and makes the reader complicit with such operations. This triple working of memory at the semantic levels of content and form and in the act of reading demands closer attention than it has enjoyed thus far, since it is the cultural/historical axis of allusion that has been privileged.[17] Moving into the field of classical reception, this is not an altogether new approach. As Hardwick, who has proposed the notion of "disremembering" to think about adaptations of the *Odyssey*, notes that "the term 'new memorysm' has been used to describe ways in which new writing uses classical material" ("Thinking with Classical Reception"19). And she expands, "Authors (ancient and modern) and readers who are familiar with earlier material join in a kind of co-authorship, creating new narratives and ways of looking at the world that are anchored in a shared (albeit constructed) memory of the classical and/or mythological past" (19). My approach is different from Hardwick's, in that I am not interested in how *Antígona* "co-authors" the past, but rather in how its playful and productive *forgetting* of the past opens spaces for the future. It is forgetting that orients us towards the future, as we will discuss later,[18] because it is in those spaces of loss that the new can intervene.[19]

Memory is also a fitting heuristic metaphor because it is linked to emotions. As Anne Carson puts it in the context of yet another take on classical reception, "remembering draws attention to lostness and is made possible by emotions of space that open backward into a void" (*Economy of the Unlost* 38). Building on Carson's suggestive metaphor, I am interested in the idea of memory as a textual activity that opens emotional spaces, empty spaces in the hypotext that can be filled affectively in the present of the hypertext. And so, this chapter claims that one way in which *Antígona* is oriented toward the future is by remembering Sophocles' *Antigone* (and "Antigone" as a body of texts) while selectively opening emotional spaces of loss in it.[20]

Making angles, opening spaces

One of the forms this productive forgetting of the hypotext, this opening of spaces of loss, takes in *Antígona* can be thought with Genette as "distribution of dramatic discourse," that is the reassigning of lines to different characters or the redistribution of is shown "on stage" (*Palimpsests* 285). In this section, I look at how Watanabe redistributes lines and whole scenes from Sophocles' *Antigone*. Redistribution, to continue with the spatial metaphor I borrow from Carson, is like forming an angle, from which some things go out of sight and others appear in the field of vision. "The character of our knowledge is always dependent on the observer's angle of vision," says Martindale in *Redeeming the Text* (2). Martindale is not talking about memory here, but I want to take his observation in this direction, adding it to Carson's, to think about how memory, as a metaphor of hypertextuality, generates "angles of vision" and creates spaces that fundamentally transform the affective and political landscape of "Antigone."

My first example is the famous line: "It is impossible to know the soul and mind and judgement of a man until they are revealed, tested by a position of power and the making of laws," said by Creon in Sophocles (Soph. *Ant.* 175–7, my translation from the Greek).[21] There, the line is colored with tragic irony—"the distance between what the protagonists expect and the disastrous way things turn out," to put it with Ian Ousby (475). For it will be Creon's own heart that will find itself put to the test as the events of the tragedy unfold.[22] Watanabe reassigns the line to the character of Antígona,[23] thus creating an angle from the Sophoclean text. Reassigned to Antígona, the line loses the tragic irony, since this character never attains power but, on the contrary, dies at the hands of the political authority. Instead, the line takes on the righteous and didactic tone of civilian protest. In contrast to the hypotext, this Antígona never speaks the "vernacular of sovereign power"—to use Judith Butler's formulation (28)—that so problematically links her to Creon in the Sophoclean version, as Butler has also argued. Rather, she speaks *to* sovereign power while staying minoritarian in her speech (as we will also see later). Without the distance created by irony, our affective engagement with the characters is affected, because we feel sympathy directly; the politics of the text are also thereby more obviously aligned with Antígona's oppressed position, rather than with the tragic tyrant. Thus, the redistribution of lines has a political and ethical effect, aligning the text with a subaltern position, or as Greenwood puts it, "in sympathy with the dispossessed" ("Subaltern Classics" 580).

My second example of how line redistribution creates angles and spaces of void in the hypotext comes in poem XIII, in which Watanabe reassigns to Antígona lines that belong to the second choral ode in Sophocles. There, the choral ode comes right after the scene where Antigone confesses her crime, rejects Ismene's help, and is sentenced to death by her uncle Creon.[24] The choral song does not focus on Antigone's particular plight but moves away from the individual character, lamenting the curse that a long time ago befell the house of the Labdacids (Soph. *Ant.* 594–6) and, even more generally, suggesting that human ruin comes from transgression of Zeus' rule (Soph. *Ant.* 604–14). By redistributing the content of the corresponding choral lines to the character of Antígona, Watanabe forgets the gnomic, more detached elements of the choral ode, homing in on Antígona's particular plight.

> The old men say that an ancient curse weighed down upon my father and mother,
> and that misfortunes, like the waves of the sea, will continue to break anew

from one generation to the next.
So, from here, though you can't hear me, old men, I
    remind you
of a law from Olympus
which says
that nothing great sets foot in the life of men
without a curse.
If *peace* is that great thing, I am the curse, the wayward wave
that breaks and dies from inside this cavern. (*Ant.* XIII, emphasis
mine)

The "old men" mentioned by Antígona are, of course, the chorus of elders in Sophocles. Specifically, Watanabe reworks the image of the breaking wave: in Sophocles, it is the "wave of sorrow" that has broken over the children of the Labdacids generation after generation. By mentioning the chorus of elders, Antígona (the character) thus makes a metatextual allusion to the Sophoclean hypotext, but there is an important twist: she self-consciously assumes in her own persona what the chorus was lamenting gnomically. *She* is the breaking wave of sorrow: "If peace is that great thing, *I* am the curse, the wayward wave/ that breaks and dies from inside this cavern" (emphasis mine). Therefore, again, as we saw with the elimination of tragic irony before, Watanabe's text reduces distance (from a universal concern to the particular) and this changes the tone of the passage: assuming this identity, Antígona moves from a politics of passive lamentation to a reparative action that seeks peace. Moreover, Antígona's self-conscious assumption of her "wayward" identity as a medium for peace introduces a theme that is missing in Sophocles, whose text is not quite concerned with "peace" but rather with (violent) victory (see Soph. *Ant.* 148).[25] Hence, the redistribution of lines from the second choral ode to the character of Antígona creates this particular angle, where a new affect appears: the *desire* for peace.[26] This new desire for "peace" connects with the opening line by the Narradora, who, as we saw, calls attention to the fact that "today is the first day of the peace." Taken together, that opening line—an innovation with respect to the Sophoclean hypotext—and the choral passage redistributed to the character of Antígona generate an affective and political landscape for the text as a whole, where the desire for peace and a politics of peace-making come to occupy the empty space of what is forgotten or lost from the Sophoclean version: namely, the status-quo voice of the chorus of elders, which orients the Sophoclean text backward. *Antígona* thus takes a wayward turn towards a future of peace.

Yet a third example is the monologue by Antígona in poem VIII. The poem/scene in Watanabe's text elaborates on the general theme of the first choral ode in Sophocles (often called the "Ode to Humans"),[27] which could be summarized along these lines: There are many awe-inspiring/strange things (*deiná*, Soph. *Ant.* 332–3), but none more than humans; they have accomplished impressive achievements, yet they have found no way out of death.[28] Watanabe's version redistributes this ode to the character of Antígona. Most of the content of the choral passage is forgotten, but the theme of human finitude is reworked. As Antígona looks at Polinices' corpse, she says:

> O gods, when you could have made us of invisible substance
>   or stone
> that needs no burial,
> why fashion us from perishable matter, from flesh
> that does not resist the invisible force of putrefaction? (*Ant.* VII)

The space of void opened with respect to the hypotext gives way to an affective speech, where it is the pain that comes from the perception of putrefaction that is rendered visible. Instead of the detached, general meditation on human nature offered by the Sophoclean chorus ("Hades alone humans did not manage to escape"),[29] we see Antígona facing the universal truth of human finitude in the very concrete corpse of her beloved brother.[30] What "happens" here is mostly an intensity of feelings as Antígona's living body encounters the "force"—to use Deleuze's term for that which affects a body, of the dead corpse of her brother.[31] As a result of the encounter with that force, Antígona wishes for a non-human existence ("when you could have made us of invisible substance or stone").[32] And this image makes yet another angle with another image in Sophocles, when in her final lament on her way to her "burial" Antigone compares herself to Niobe, a mythical figure who turned into stone (Soph. *Ant.* 825–31). The name of Niobe is forgotten in Watanabe's monologue assigned to Antígona, but the non-human becoming remains in his imagery with the mention of the stone. Yet while Sophocles' heroine only likens her death to that of the mythical figure, in Watanabe the comparison expands into a *desire* for an inanimate form of existence that escapes the pains of finitude (the "invisible force of putrefaction"). This painful wish serves only to highlight her self-consciousness that her body is a "tragic body," to use Nancy Worman's phrasing, who defines them as having "beginnings and ends, show[ing] the passage of time … subject to incursion, vulnerable in many regards. They also expose existential boundaries and their undoings" (*Tragic Bodies* 6–7).

Thus, while forgetting Niobe and the Greek mythical backdrop, this version renews the tragic element through its approach to desire and embodiment. It meets tragedy at the point of tragic embodiment (as defined by Worman) and from that point makes an angle that forgets myth and opens an affective space: the desire of becoming non-human, inflected by the painful entanglement with the mortal body of an other.

Having looked at the angles and spaces generated by line redistribution, I want now to look briefly at what I call, expanding on Genette's concepts, the distribution of sympathies. Whereas Sophocles is interested in the ambiguity of the conflict and provides emotional and rational elements for the audience to sympathize both with Antigone and Creon,[33] Watanabe's *Antígona* distributes our sympathies away from the king and towards Antígona and Ismene. This is achieved, formally, through a quantitative reduction of the play, performing on the hypotext what Genette calls "excision" and "condensation" (*Palimpsests* 229 and 237, respectively). Watanabe's *Antígona* condenses long dialogues into a few lines; sometimes what is left of a scene or choral song is only a brief allusion. Significantly, it also excises Sophocles' last scene, in which Eurydice (Creon's unlucky wife) first hears of her son Haemon's suicide, then kills herself off stage (Soph. *Ant.* 1182–316). In Sophocles, this is followed by a short dialogue (also excised in this version) between Creon and the chorus, where the bereaved king laments his mistake and fate. In fact, the character of Eurydice is completely absent from Watanabe's version. These excisions bear considerably on the way in which this hypertext makes meaning and engages readers' sympathies. In Genette's analysis, condensation and excision are considered "purely quantitative" transformations "without thematic incidence" (228). Yet by subtracting the death of Eurydice from the tragedy and eliminating the pathetic dialogue between Creon and the chorus that ensues, the hypertext becomes less of Creon's tragedy, shifting the affective weight to Antígona and Ismene and also situating its politics as decidedly anti-oppression.

The redistribution of sympathies is also enforced through a change in the order the events of the tragedy are presented. The Sophoclean opening scene with Antigone and Ismene, where the two sisters discuss Antigone's plan to burry Polyneices and Ismene refuses to help, is moved to the end and thus comes to occupy precisely the position occupied by the excised scene of Eurydice's death. This substitution of one scene for the other further signals that this is the *sisters'* tragedy and that *we* are not aligning our sympathy with the oppressor.[34]

Other spaces of void are opened and never filled, and that omission is also meaningful *as such*. Conspicuous elements that are left out of the picture—productively forgotten—in *Antígona*, though they have played important roles in *Antigone*'s reception history. One important instance is the Greek adjective *deinós* (δεινός), which I translated as "awe-inspiring/ strange" in my summary of the Sophoclean "Ode to Humans" mentioned above ("There are many awe-inspiring/strange things..."). Sophocles' characterization of human beings as *deinoí* has been the object of important thought in psychoanalytic (e.g. Lacan) and political theory (e.g. Žižek) as well as in philosophy (e.g. Heidegger). As Tina Chanter notes, Lacan, Žižek, and Heidegger (after Hölderlin) translate *deinós* as "uncanny" (*unheimlich* in German) and transfer the epithet from the chorus' general meditation on humankind to Antigone herself, making of *her* the uncanny (19–21). In Chanter's words, these readings posit Antigone "as that which is to be expelled, as a disruptive force whose harmful potential must be reined in for the preservation of the stability of the social order" (22). In contrast to these readings, as Chanter also notes, "stands a remarkably varied tradition of translations and adaptations that draw inspiration from the figure of Antigone as a radical political resource" (22). For instance, one well-known adaptation that does this is *The Island*, by South African playwright Athol Fugard. It renders *deinós* as "monstrous" and uses it to qualify not Antigone nor humanity but the system of apartheid. With this word choice, Fugard clearly takes a postcolonial position that explicitly locates the hypertext in its geopolitical context. In stark contrast with this history of reception of the "strange" quality of Antigone, Watanabe leaves the issue of *deinós* completely off the page. As we saw, of the second Sophoclean chorus where the adjective appears (here reassigned to Antígona), only the theme of human finitude is left, and not as a general meditation, but as the concrete, very particular encounter of Antígona with the putrefying corpse of her brother (an encounter that Sophocles leaves off the page). Instead of signaling the strangeness of her claim and how it disrupts a presumed community, this text focuses on her body in pain as locus of political failure.

Another essential element in the reception of Sophocles' *Antigone* that is completely forgotten in Watanabe's *Antígona* is the characters' famous and, to use Simon Goldhill's characterization of it (after Buxton), "baffling"[35] formulation of the *nomos* (law or custom) on which she founds her act against Creon's prohibition to bury Polyneices' corpse. In Sophocles, this is how the heroine pronounces her "law":

> I would have never taken on this labor, in defiance of the citizens, if I had been the mother of children or if my husband, having died, were a putrefying corpse. According to what law do I say this? If a husband

had died, there would be another one for me; and a child could be
born from another husband, if I lost one. But with my mother and
father in Hades, no brother could ever blossom again for me. (Soph.
Ant. 905–12, my translation from the Greek)

The account that the heroine offers of her law is problematic on many
accounts, but the essential contradiction, which makes it impossible to el-
evate her reasoning to universal law, is that she claims the superiority of
kinship over political relationships while at the same time undercutting
the notion of kinship when she claims that her rationale applies only in the
exceptional case of the brother (and of *this* brother alone, as Ismene is con-
spicuously left out of the picture, nor is it clear that she would have done
it for Eteocles). I cannot survey here the long history of interpretations of
this passage and of this contradiction, which has proven so productive for
political, ethical, feminist, queer, and psychoanalytical theories. Instead, I
will briefly engage Judith Butler's reading of it in *Antigone's Claim*, deeply
engaged as it is with the most influential interpretations that came before
it and enormously influential in turn; as such, it is instructive of many of
the issues understood to be at stake here. Butler focuses primarily on Hegel's and Lacan's important readings of the Greek tragedy, which are two
"forms of idealized kinship." In Hegel's interpretation, says Butler, "Antigone represents the laws of kinship, the household gods" (28). The contradiction lies in that her insistence "on representing those laws is precisely
what constitutes a crime in another more public order of law" (29). Lacan,
on his part, Butler posits, locates Antigone "at the threshold of the symbolic, understood as the linguistic register in which kinship relations are
instated and maintained," her death "precipitated precisely by the symbolic
insupportability of her desire" (29). Reworking aspects of both readings,
Butler questions whether Antigone's death is "precisely a limit that requires
to be read as that operation of political power that forecloses what forms
of kinship will be intelligible, what kinds of lives can be countenanced as
living" (29). Her position is that Antigone disrupts structures of kinship
(rather than representing them or being unsupported by them, as in Hegel
and Lacan) and that her disruption opens up, rather than forecloses, the
possibility of making intelligible other forms of living.

   Notably, Watanabe does not include the troubling argument in Antígona's speeches, taking a turn away from the long tradition of readings that
have put the emphasis on Antigone's "law." In this hypertext, Antígona
mentions the "unwritten laws of the gods" as a guiding principle of her
act, but the "baffling" rationale with which Sophocles' character tries to

unpack what she means by those unwritten laws is completely missing. Thus, in poem/scene XI, as she confronts Creonte, the heroine says:

> You say
> I have broken your law. Do you,
> a mortal, expect to prevail
> over the unwritten but unbreakable laws
> of
> They alone have power over the bodies of the dead.
> Remember it: they alone. (*Ant*. XI)

She is not concerned with the irreplaceability of Polinices that troubles her argument in Sophocles and that is so important in both Lacan and Butler's readings. What concerns her is only his equal right for burial, as she makes clear in poem/scene X:

> For every death I want a funeral,
> and then,
> then,
> then,
> oblivion. (*Ant*. X)

The temporal adverb: "then, then, then," opens space and time, displacing from view Antigone's law of irreplaceability and postponing to the future the forgetting of every dead of the war. It forgets one thing in order to open space for a new injunction against oblivion, so that the text commits not to Polinices' irreplaceability but to a universal justice for all the fallen. This version thus obliquely restitutes the universality that is so bafflingly asserted yet at the same time missing in Antigone's claim.

The monologue: affective landscapes

The redistributions and omissions we have looked at in the previous section need to be understood *beside* another formal frame: the alternating use of monologue and narration. In transforming *Antígona* into a text that oscillates between monologue and narration, Watanabe performs upon the Greek source what Genette calls an "intramodal transformation" (*Palimpsests* 284ff.), which takes place when the hypertext retains the same genre (in this case, tragedy) but changes the mode of representation of the hypotext (in this case, dialogue).[36] I refrain from getting into issues of genre but am interested here in *Antígona*'s forgetting of modes of representation and its use of poems in the form of monologues.[37] As a result of forgetting dialogue, a very important poetic device in Sophocles (and Greek drama in general), known as "stichomythia" or "line for line dialogue," is notably left out. This formal decision has important consequences for the meaning of the text as well as its affective and political landscapes. I believe this is one of *Antígona*'s most important gestures, for the use of monologues shapes the spaces that the text gives to either action or feeling, especially generating the space for an internal view of the characters that is lacking in the Sophoclean version. In this section, I look at the effects of eliminating dialogue and at the spaces of feeling that the monologues open up in the hypotext.

In a chapter devoted specifically to the significance of stichomythia in Sophocles, Simon Goldhill argues that stichomythia is meaningful in itself, as it makes evident "the fissures of language, the multiple obscurities and tensions of civic discourse, as a defining aspect of the genre as a civic event" (79). Moreover, he argues that this form of dramatic dialogue in Sophocles, which often falls into "fragmented miscommunication" (78), instead of standing as the "ideal for the political process and as a token of civilized life," "uncovers the potential naïvety in such idealism" (80). According to Goldhill, Sophocles exploits this form not to show communication at work, but at its weakest, failing points.

If we think now of what Watanabe does with the monologue, something similar can be observed. Curiously, by eliminating dialogue, Watanabe's text takes to the extreme the effect of isolation that one can see in the miscommunication of Sophocles' characters noted by Goldhill. Thus, the formal change works to somehow revitalize the effect of the form that is left out of the frame. If stichomythia shows the failure of democratic politics in the fissures of language, as Goldhill argues, the monologue in Watanabe's *Antígona* shows isolation as an effect of a failed political community.

The fact that characters never engage in dialogue is one of the most striking formal features of encountering *Antígona* as a reader. Characters never seem to be present at the same time—except in the sequence of monologues by Creonte and Hemón in poem XIV, where the two characters somewhat address each other, and their lines threaten to bleed into dialogue without becoming one, thereby mirroring their failure to meet each other halfway. The "action" of the text unfolds soliloquy after soliloquy, or one could even say, lyric poem after lyric poem.[38] "Action," strictly speaking, always happens behind the scenes in the text, in the ellipsis between poem and poem, monologue and monologue. Characters do not "do" anything, other than talking. Because of this, Laura Alonso argues that narrating constitutes the only action of this play. Yet I would argue that it is not only narration that "happens." For, while it is true that the final revelation of the Narradora retrospectively turns the text into a narrative, looked at from the progression of the temporality of reading (or spectating), the talking that the individual characters do—each assigned their individual name and never completely subsumed under the voice of the Narradora—also "happens." In fact, their monological words are what happen preeminently, as we spend most of the time intimating with the characters' monological thoughts, which only at times convey a clear sense of action.

Exploiting the poetic possibilities of the monologue, Watanabe constantly focuses on moments of the story that are not shown in the scenes of Sophocles' *Antigone*, yet another kind of redistribution that opens up spaces of feeling and action.[39] For instance, as we saw in poem/scene X, Antígona appears in the very act of burying Polinices and addresses the corpse in a particularly affective monologue, that is at the same time a meditation on human finitude and an intense moment of desire for becoming non-human. In Sophocles, the burial takes place off stage, during the time that elapses between the first arrival of a guard in front of Creon and the second time the guard appears, now with Antigone in shackles (Soph. *Ant.* 223ff. and 407ff.). Watanabe imagines the omitted scene and intervenes in its Greek hypotext to represent the inside of the plot, entering the recesses to give us back a view from within, folding it inside out.[40] Omission and reimagining are, of course, typical hypertextual gestures,[41] as Hardwick similarly observes in her reading of receptions of an episode of the *Odyssey* ("Thinking with Classical Reception" 15). Yet what is interesting about this particular take on omission and reimagining is the use of the monologues as recesses opened in the hypotext to get closer to the feelings of the characters.[42]

Particularly fleshy and filled with feelings are the monologues spoken by Antígona, where we see the fragile side of this heroine, whom we are used to imagining as ferocious,[43] single-minded, and often even unsympathetic.[44] Contrary to her Greek counterpart, who is always in the company of the chorus during her lament (Soph. *Ant.* 806–943), this Antígona appears extremely isolated and lonely. Loneliness, of course, is not altogether Watanabe's invention. In Sophocles, although the character is accompanied by the chorus, in her final dirge she is painfully aware that she leaves the world alone, which the text represents using a series of what are usually called "privative adjectives" (without fame, friendless, unwed);[45] and, on several occasions, the character also complains that no friend is mourning her death (ll. 847, 881, and 919). However, Watanabe's text delves into this, not by exploiting the semantic field of referentiality (like the adjectives in Sophocles that directly mean solitude) but by inserting loneliness into the very form of the text with the use of the monologue.[46]

The representation of loneliness and isolation in strikingly bodily terms is something that Watanabe's text shares with ancient Greek tragedy as a genre, whose "dominant aesthetic experience," as Worman puts it, is precisely the viewing of the body in pain (*Tragic Bodies* 13). Yet, as Worman also notes, in Greek tragedy

> displaying bodies in pain conforms to a gendered scheme that matches the political reality, treating male bodies as more valued public objects and more worthy of focus, mourning, and celebration, while female bodies tend to either mediate or focalize this attention or to be effectively quarantined in offstage interior spaces. (*Tragic Bodies* 15)

In fact, in Sophocles' *Antigone* in particular, we never get to see Antigone in physical pain. Thus, the representation of Antígona's body in pain both meets Sophocles at a point of tragic aesthetics and also makes a gender-inflected angle. For instance, the text represents the extreme loneliness and the bodily pain of Antígona inside of the cave/tomb: "Darkness detaches my body from its reality./ I am/ only when I feel my skin or touch the rough stone of the cavern" (*Ant.* XIII). The monologue renders visible how loneliness casts painful doubts upon the very existence of the self; it speaks of life and consciousness reduced to the haptic perception of the skin and the stone, suggesting a continuity between bodies that echoes Antígona's earlier desire to become "invisible substance or stone" when facing Polinices' corpse, as we saw. Thus, it also makes the physical pain of the human body reverberate and expand on the non-human surfaces of the landscape. In stark contrast to the "offstage quarantine" of female characters signals by Worman, in this version Antígona's body in pain is not only rendered visible but also extensively so. For while in Sophocles, the heroine disappears after the dirge that ends in line 943, Watanabe keeps her with us almost until the end, and we witness the slow death of the heroine throughout three different poems/scenes: XIII, XV, and XIX. I have already quoted XIII, where we see the character's physical awareness of the cessation of her biological life (see pages 109–10 above). In XIX, it is the Narradora who imagines Antígona's torment in quite fleshly terms:

I see her waiting for an impossible drop of water to form
on the arid rock
and fall in her *thirsty mouth*,
or *groping* in that forbidding world for a bitter green
to ease her infinite *hunger*,
or *muttering slow words*, so that her own *voice*
    accompanies her,
while *her body falls into a lethargy
folding forward like a wax figurine*. (*Ant.* XIX, emphases mine)

The poem insists upon the bodily elements of thirst, hunger, voice, exhaustion, and melting. This emphasis on the body continues later in the same poem, when we come back to the voice of Antígona and read the heroine describing her own vanishing, almost like a transformation into another form of non-human matter, into light:[47]

What I saw was different,
I wanted to *enter that light and dissolve in its nimble quality.*
Oh, if only that were the road to step into Hades, and I
were a *sudden light, a body withdrawn from this torture*
long and perverse. (*Ant.* XIX, emphases mine)

I emphasized the affective elements that the text uses to construct the image of the title character's slow death: the thirsty mouth; the anxious hand groping on the wall of the cave; the hunger; the slow words produced by the voice; her own voice that turns into a sort of other, allowing her to have some consciousness; the body that folds and melts as if it were wax; and the desire for dissolution into nimble light. I want to connect this affective landscape with the formal change from dialogue to monologue I am tracking in this section. Going back to Goldhill and his argument about stichomythia—how it shows the failures of communication and, more broadly, of the political project of democracy itself—let us contrast what happens in *Antígona* with the intimate, affective, and extensive representation of her pain in the monologues. With the change of form and the opening of a different affective landscape, language does not so much show the failure of communication Goldhill signals in Sophocles as it shows the lived experience of the catastrophic failure of politics, lived on the very skin of the citizens. Put a bit differently, language here shows us the flesh of political failure.

This opening of an affective space that renders visible the flesh of a failed political community in the body of a female character could also be extended to (*beside*) the rest of the characters' monologues. The monologues show us not only the heroine's solitude but that of every character. In fact, everyone in *Antígona* is monumentally alone. Solitude is revealed as one of the invisible yet painfully tangible experiences of a post-war time. For instance, let us look at Creonte. Sophocles shows us a Creon whose layers unfold as the tragedy progresses until, at the end, he is left alone. There, Creon's solitude is most visible at the very end of the play, when on top of the deaths of Antigone and Haemon, he learns about his wife Eurydice's suicide. It is in that final and late moment when the king feels, at last, the burden of his own blindness. Watanabe, as I've said, simplifies the story and gets rid of Eurydice. The text shows the loneliness of the king even before the double death of his son and niece. In poem XVII, the Narradora, as if looking at Creonte from a rear window, says:

> No one around. Creonte is sitting alone in the center
> of the great hall.
> He looks at himself in the mirror
> and sees a vexed man drinking wine.
> And no one around.
> The wine comes from the royal vines,
> but his thoughts fall into the glass and distort the drink.
> And no one around. (*Ant.* XVII)

The contrast between the single figure and the monumental room; the reflected image of the self in the drink; the thought that materializes to multiply the self, thus populating its emptiness with even more self-reflective solitude; and the repetition of "no one around" all mark the loneliness of this character. Yet, contrary to what we saw in the case of Antígona in poem/scene X, where it's the force of the perception of Polinices' corpse that triggers her desire to transcend human finitude, nothing links Creonte's affects to the deaths of others. In this sense, this Creonte is unlike the Sophoclean tyrant, whose despair we start to see only after Haemon's death: "Oh, brokenhearted, I've learned," he says in response to the chorus when they tell him that he acted too late (Soph. *Ant.* 1270–2, my translation). In Watanabe's version, the tyrant seems to be always already isolated. Thus, as I claimed before, the text aligns our sympathies with the minoritarian figures in the text (mostly the female victim and the female survivor: Antígona and Ismene). However, by exploiting the capacity of the monologue to portray

Creonte's solitude, the text adds a certain complexity and avoids being cartoonish and pamphleteer, while not going as far as asking us to empathize or identify with the character representing oppressive power. Loneliness and isolation appear as the primary texture in this broken political landscape, embodied not only on the body of a female character but embedded in the entire fabric of the fissured community. Through the focus on flesh, on physicality, and on the surfaces of things language conveys the solitude of the tyrant, the other side of the coin of political failure.[48]

The Narradora's loneliness is dual. Her figure evokes the Messenger of Greek tragedy as well as the chorus, who like her is present through the entire play and who, just as her narration does, weaves together the separate scenes announcing characters' entrances and shaping audiences' expectations with their introductory comments. But again, when this text meets tragedy at a formal point, it makes an angle and twists both the form and content of the hypotext. For one, the Narradora speaks from an individual position that cannot be taken as that of a unified body of members of the community, like the Greek chorus. This sense of isolation is made even more acute by the fact that for most of the play the Narradora seems to be talking to herself, not addressing a specific audience, whereas in Greek tragedy the Messenger and the chorus always address an internal audience. This makes more meaningful the contrasting two moments when the Narradora explicitly addresses an audience of Thebans ("The guilt we feel is within us, Thebans" IV and "People of Thebes" XI) who remain otherwise silent and invisible throughout.

But the Narradora's complete loneliness and isolation is revealed in the last monologue. Unlike the last scene from Sophocles, where Creon receives the news of Eurydice's death, Watanabe closes the tragedy with a monologue by the Narradora in which she reveals her identity and acknowledges her silent role in the tragic events she has just narrated. She is Ismene, left alone on the stage and in the world of the story, now that her three siblings have died. Full of remorse because she did not help Antígona, nor was she able to save her, Ismene confesses her own torment:

> In your elevated kingdom
> ask Polinices to forgive me for the duty I did not do at the right time
> because I shrank in *the furrowed face of power*, and tell him
> that already I have a heavy punishment:
> to remember, every day, your *deed*,
> which *tortures*
> and *brings me to shame*. (*Ant.* XXII, emphases mine)

Her solitude, again, is not told directly or referentially, but we see it through affects and feelings. Ismene's language is markedly affective: her fear to help her sister is described as a sensorial reaction ("shrank") to a sensorially perceived abstraction ("the furrowed face of power"); it is the memory of her sister's deed (the word in Spanish, "gesto," also means "expression" or even "countenance") that she feels as torture and which causes the feeling of shame. Ismene's affective language thus also shows the bodily aspect of political failure.

And so, as the story comes to an end, each and every character has been revealed in their isolation and loneliness, and their speeches remain isolated and fragmentary pieces in the memory of Ismene who, unable to bring cohesion to a broken community, can only re-imagine and represent the pain of the dead, for others to feel. Loneliness in the aftermath of war, then, is the feeling and texture that predominantly occupies the spaces opened up by the angles that *Antígona* takes from the hypotext through the formal change from dialogue to monologue and through a careful engagement with the bodily and affective experiences of the characters.

Hands-on narration: a reparative gesture

If the monologue opens up a view especially to the affects and emotions of the characters, to the loneliness and isolation as the textures of a failed political community, narration provides a reparative path. It could be said that Ismene's main "action" in this version is that of narrating. Alonso, as I mentioned above, proposes that the very act of narrating constitutes the main action, not only of the character of Ismene but of Watanabe's *Antígona* as a whole. Yet I disagree with Alonso that narrating constitutes the sole action of Watanabe's *Antígona*, as I already argued when signaling the importance of the monologue and its opening of affective spaces. I now add that, as the Narradora reveals her identity as Ismene in the last poem/scene, she goes beyond narration and *actually performs* the funerary rites for Polinices. This, as Robles Moreno's reading suggests, is the main action of this text ("Yo soy la hermana"). This final ritual, I propose, can be read as a reparative gesture and is linked to the text's general attention to the force of affects. Following the thread of my argument, I'm interested first, in how the use of narration aligns this text with postmodern dramaturgical practices, and then, in how the gender inflection of the Narradora is a formal and a thematic intervention into—an angle taken with respect to—Sophocles' *Antigone* (and as always, "Antigone") that is key to the text's minoritarian position, its reparative gesture, and its orientation towards the future.

I am not convinced that Watanabe's *Antígona* comfortably wears the "postdramatic" epithet (see pp. 3–5 above). As I argued, Yuyachkani's "Third Theatre" practices ought to be understood within the global context of postmodern theater, especially as it concerns the dehierarchization of the written text over other, non-verbal, forms of constructing meaning on stage, which converges with Lehman's concept of the postdramatic. But when we think of Watanabe's text as separate from the performance, we can see how Yuyachkani's and Watanabe's aesthetics differ—and thus ask to be thought of differently. Watanabe's text is quite conventional in its plot-driven use of suspense, one of its main literary strategies, as the entire text is built around the climactic moment that comes in the last poem, where the Narradora reveals that she has been Ismene all long. This characteristic directly clashes with Lehman's conceptualization of the postdramatic, as we saw.[49] That said, as I also argued in the Introduction, Lehman's concept is built exclusively around the study of theater practitioners and writers from Europe and the United States, so I think it would be equally wrong to fail to situate Watanabe's use of narration within contemporary and post-modern poetic sensibilities (if not necessarily "postdramatic" in Lehman's sense). Moreover, recent work on classical reception has pointed out the important role that recreations of Greek drama have played in the development of (European) postdramatic theater,[50] making it all the more important to situate Watanabe's (and Yuyachkani's) *Antígona* within the broader context of experimental postmodern theater engagements with Greek tragedy, as I also argued in my Introduction. Even though it does not quite fit Lehman's Eurocentric notion, *Antígona* is neither a traditional drama in the sense Lehman opposes to the "postdramatic."[51] The fragmented form of discourse and the blurring of genres—by now a given of postmodern poetics, where "the borders between literary genres have become fluid" (*A Poetics* 9)—are particularly notable. In fact, one wonders how to categorize the text: is this text a polyphonic lyric poem, is it a play?[52] One could even ask, is it still a tragedy?

If postmodernist poetics is characterized, broadly speaking and among other things, by a critical, as opposed to nostalgic, integration, and interrogation of the past in the present, where the aesthetic forms and social formations of the past "are problematized by critical reflection," as Hutcheon (*A Poetics* 4) proposes, I submit that this text is quietly postmodern. It exercises a quiet critique of an ancient text, mostly through formal decisions, through incisions, cuts, and angles, as I have been arguing (and thinking of mostly in terms of "forgetting") in this chapter. The criticism never announces itself out loud, it is never thematized, and the text eschews irony (that quintessential postmodern device).[53] The text eschews metanarrative (perhaps the most important contribution of postmodern thought)[54] precisely by focalizing the story through the narrative voice of a minor character, Ismene, and presents the events decidedly from *one* (minoritarian) perspective. Thus, it gestures toward the text's positionality, that is, it renders visible that it is "derived from complex networks of local or contingent conditions" (*A poetics* 12).

With Ismene's contingent position as the narrator of the play, Watanabe's version accomplishes something along the lines of what Catherine Holland's feminist reading asks us to do as interpreters of Sophocles' tragedy: to "*establish our present as different from the past*, to put an end to past inegalitarian, exclusionary doctrines and practices that make feminism appear impossible" (40, emphasis mine). The new Ismene, with her new political action, does not belong to the ancient text and its past tense. Ismene introduces a difference into the narrative we continue to tell ourselves through the filter of ancient myth. Her difference ought to be understood within a feminist framework, to the extent that it reframes the story of the myth as one told and repaired by a female survivor. This survivor generates not only a narrative as a means to resist oppressive power's insistence on forgetting catastrophe but also a ritual that seeks to repair the conditions of that very oppressive power, effectively establishing "our present as different from the past."

This reparative gesture takes place in the last poem/scene and, as we will see, is assemblage by sensory imagery and, especially, by Ismene's hands, as they change from a hand-tied position to one of caring for. As I mentioned before, what in Sophocles' *Antigone* is the first scene—the dialogue between the two sisters in which Antigone informs Ismene of Creon's edict and tells her about her plans to go against the edict and bury Polyneices, asking her to join her in the deed—comes at the end in Watanabe's text. In this last poem/scene, the Narradora reveals that she is Ismene, "the sister who was hand-tied by fear." She narrates the encounter with her now dead sister and her refusal to participate in Polinices' burial at that time. Let us look at the monologue and narration more carefully:

NARRADORA

The deaths of this story come to me
not so that I make a trade of telling other people's misfortunes.
They come to me, and so vividly, because they are my own

misfortune:
I'm the sister who was hand-tied by fear.
Antígona came into my house like a furious sudden flash
and spoke to me: "Ismene,
I want your hands to help me bury the corpse of
our beloved brother,
I trust
that, born noble,
you have not turned petty."
Her words were seething
but I had the spirit of a little animal,
huddled up,
and knowing that reason tended her
I said she was raving, that a blow of madness had struck
    her head.
It was fear, Antígona, because death would be our penalty
    for burying him.
Come, my sister, I begged you, let us rather ask the dead
    to excuse us
and let the orders of the living powers
    prevail,
but you rebuked me, saying: "You, Ismene, seek
assent from the world of the tyrant, I'll go after the favor
of the gods," and left
for the hill of our dead. (*Ant.* XXII)

In changing the order of the scene, putting it at the end, and having it
narrated instead of acted, Watanabe's text takes an important angle with
respect to Sophocles', turning the entire text retrospectively into a memory. But this final poem/scene also does something more. As Ismene utters
these words, she is performing the belated funeral rite for her brother:

> *(She unwraps something and uncovers Polinices' mortuary mask.*
> *After each stanza, she offers a libation.)*
> Antígona,
> do you see this world below?
> The palace now bears the silence of a mausoleum
> and from there we are ruled by a breathing corpse, a king,
> tormented,
> who grows old swiftly.

Dear sister, look:
this is the face of our brother as it was before the dogs
and the vultures and putrefaction,
and these late libations are from my little spirit full of remorse.

In your elevated kingdom
ask Polinices to forgive me for the duty I did not do at the right time
because I shrank in the furrowed face of power, and tell him
that I already have a heavy punishment:
to remember, every day, your deed,
which tortures
and brings me to shame. (*Ant.* XXII)

With this action, Ismene becomes something *more* than a narrator: she becomes politicized.[55] She becomes an agent of change against an antipolitics of isolation in the post-war society. With her refusal to forget the dead, her insistence that *every* dead gets a funeral, she enacted, to put it with Fradinger, "the memory of the political," "a memory of the antagonism that constitutes the political sphere" ("Demanding the Political" 68). But with her burial ritual, she adds to (*beside*) antagonism the politics of reparation. With these gestures, Ismene's political position changes drastically, from a passive witness of atrocity whose silence makes her complicit with oppression, to a politicized agent of change. Moreover, when she says, "It was fear, Antígona, because death would be our penalty for burying him," the text echoes the ways in which Ismene has been traditionally received in the corpus of "Antigone" (as a coward),[56] but as she performs the ritual she goes beyond those interpretations by repairing fear with memory and care.

By "reparation" I do not mean that the ritual brings reconciliation to society in the sense that now citizens can be at ease with their passive role as witnesses of a catastrophe inflicted on "others." To think of it along Sedgwick, this politics asserts that things do not have to remain the same. As she writes, a reparative reader can experience surprise and the past as a different possibility:

> because the reader has room to realize that the future may be different from the present, it is also possible for her to entertain such profoundly painful, profoundly relieving, ethically crucial possibilities as that the past, in turn, could have happened differently from the way it actually did. (146)

A reparative position then simultaneously (*beside*) links two seemingly contradictory emotions: the *pain* with respect to the traumatic past and the *hope* that organizes the present (which is the future with respect to the past) with a different energy, one that *cares* to do things differently and that does not, to use Holland's phrase, "reinstate the past." The surprising revelation of the Narradora's identity as Ismene in the last poem/scene establishes such a contradictory politics of pain with respect to the past and hope with respect to the present/future, a hope that is materialized in concrete reparative gestures such as narration and ritual.

In *Antígona*, aesthetic elements come into play for this reparation. The literary text (or for that matter, the performance) as an aesthetic artifact uses narration and sensorial elements to bring about such transformation. For one, what allows or triggers this reparation are the *images* that come back to Ismene and make her *tell* the story and perform the symbolic ritual of burial: "The deaths of this story come to me…," she says in poem XXII quoted above. Here Ismene privileges the visual element as she envisions the *images* of the story that come to her "so vividly." Yet this privileging of the sense of (imaginary) sight is already synesthetic, because it has been implicated throughout the narration of the entire play with the fleshy experiences in the monologues by the other characters, which she just narrated.[57] Through these other sensorial elements, she is not only a voice and a pair of eyes that envisions and witnesses, but also a body tied to the bodies of her story, deeply implicated in it. This assemblage of entangled bodies becomes completed in the text when she uncovers and holds Polinices' mortuary mask in her hands and becomes literally entangled with (the material representation of) the body of her brother.

Furthermore, the Narradora's revelation of her identity as Ismene directly links to her hands her "becoming a sister" (Moro 123), as opposed to being an anonymous narrator: "I'm the sister who was hand-tied by fear."[58] Hands, as has been noted by scholars, are quite important in Sophocles' *Antigone*.[59] Valentina Moro highlights that the sororal tie between Antigone and Ismene is embodied and visible in the hand imagery used by Antigone in the opening dialogue in Sophocles: "Will you join your hand to mine in order to lift this corpse?" (Soph. *Ant.* 43).[60] Watanabe reproduces that initial mention of the hand in Antígona's line as reported by Ismene ("I want your hands to help me bury the corpse of our beloved brother") and also echoes or evokes it when Ismene reveals her identity ("hand-tied by fear"). In Sophocles, Ismene is the only member of the family that never does anything with her hands—more specifically, as Stefani Engelstein notes, "she alone in her family escapes using her hands as tools of murder or suicide" ("Sibling Logic" 51). Watanabe picks up on the Oedipal hand-play and grounds Ismene's change of identity and spirit (from anonymous narrator to implicated sister, from passive witnessing to a reparative practice) precisely in her hands: before, she was "hand-tied" (*maniatada*) by fear, now she performs with her hands the symbolic funerary rites for Polinices. As the stage directions indicate, she unwraps the mortuary mask and offers libations, both actions that imply the hands. This angle taken by Ismene's hands signals the angle taken by the text towards a different politics and ethics.

In fact, the gendered inflection of this narrator's voice, this focalizing of the story through a female, "marginal" or "ex-centric" character,[61] tracks with recent turns towards the figure of Ismene in the scholarship and creative recreations of "Antigone." It anticipates an expanding interest in the figure of the forlorn sister by feminists and political theorists concerned with ethics. The second decade of the twenty-first century has seen multiple theoretical and creative efforts, particularly by feminists, to reread the politics and ethics of "Antigone" through a revaluation of Ismene's choices and actions in Sophocles (and in the Theban plays more broadly as well as in receptions of "Antigone").[62] Bonnie Honig's feminist reading of "Antigone" opened the gates for this renovated interest in Ismene. In the article "Ismene's Forced Choice" and the book *Antigone, Interrupted*, Honig proposes that a political, feminist, reading of "Antigone" can be carved out of a different interpretation of the relationship between the two sisters. This relationship has usually been thought of in terms of an active vs. passive sister.[63] Yet against this interpretation, Honig proposes two important points. First, she reads the Sophoclean texts looking for ambiguities that allow her to argue that Ismene actually performed the first "burial" (throwing dust on the cadaver of Polyneices), without Antigone's knowledge. More productively, perhaps, she also proposes that there is an active, ethical decision on Ismene's part, when she "decides" to go on living (*Antigone, Interrupted* 33). Honig sees a concerted "sororal" action between the two sisters, in which Antigone, with her sacrifice, gives Ismene the gift of life. Antigone, says Honig, "ultimately sacrifices herself not just for the disgraced 'ungrievable' (as Butler puts it) dead brother but also for a living equal: her sister" ("Ismene's Forced Choice" 34). Thus, Honig reads "Antigone" against the grain of psychoanalysis, post-structuralism, and new humanisms like Butler's, looking for what she calls a politics of "natality," as opposed to an ethics centered around finitude and grief. "If we are going to endlessly reperform the gesture of turning to Antigone versus Oedipus," she submits, "we need a different Antigone, one who does not just immerse us in a politics of lamentation premised on shared finitude but also inaugurates *an insurgent politics of lamentation that solicits out of us a potentially shared natality*" (*Antigone, Interrupted* 85, emphasis mine).

What Honig here calls "an insurgent politics of lamentation that solicits out of us a potentially shared natality" is, in my view, what Watanabe's *Antígona* does with Ismene's hands' reparative ritual. However, it should be noted that Watanabe's take on Ismene is different from Honig's (and other feminist readings that follow in her steps) in important ways.[64] For one, Ismene clearly confesses in her last monologue that she *did not* help Antígona, nor did she perform the first burial, as Honig wants to read Sophocles. Interestingly enough, the scene that grounds Honig's reading is forgotten in Watanabe's version. In the Sophoclean scene, when the two sisters are confronted by Creon, Ismene attempts to share the blame with Antigone and thus die with her, but the heroic sister denies and rejects the complicity, claiming that her death "will be enough" (Soph. *Ant*. 547). In Watanabe's rewriting, the only encounter between the two sisters is the one I already mentioned: the last poem/scene, which is a version of Sophocles' first scene. In that last poem/scene, Ismene never mentions an encounter with Creonte in which she showed solidarity with her sister wanting to share the blame and die with her. Much to the contrary, as we saw, she confesses that she was frightened and now feels guilty and ashamed of her cowardice. Her "sorority" does not take place during the events of the tragedy (as Honig reads Sophocles) but rather in its immediate aftermath. She acknowledges that her action comes late and is motivated by regret ("and these late libations are from my little spirit full of remorse").

Yet, despite these important differences, one significant aspect that this version of *Antigone* shares with Honig and most feminist readings of the play of the last decade is its orientation towards the future. Mary Rawlinson, in one of the earliest essays to turn to a revaluation of Ismene's (and Antigone's) role, puts the *need* for this futurity thus: "Neither feminist philosophy, which is to say philosophy, *nor the future* can afford heroines who value the purity of their own conscience or abstract principle over the claims of a living sister" ("Antigone and Ismene" 105, emphasis mine). To close this section, I want to tie in this orientation towards the future with the affective turn of Ismene's narrative which I signaled above in my close reading.

Ismene's shift from being hand-tied to handling the story and the situation (as narrator first, then as agent of burial) is linked to a specific affect, that of shame.[65] This brings us back to the thread of my argument that it is the affective spaces opened up by the angles that this hypertext makes with respect to *Antigone* (and "Antigone") that imbue it with differential meaning, aesthetics, and politics. As shame moves Ismene both beyond her previous inability to act (hand-tied by fear) and beyond the borders of the action of the hypotext (burying Polinices after all the events of the received tragedy have unfolded), this "negative" feeling has a positive, reparative effect. Silvan Tomkins, one of the leading psychologists to theorize affects (and on whom Sedgwick grounds much of her work), defines shame as a negative affect activated by "the incomplete reduction of interest or joy" (*A Silvan Tomkins Handbook* 66). And he points out that, as their incomplete reaction, this negative affect is thus closely linked to the positive affects of interest-excitement and enjoyment-joy. As Donald Nathanson, commenting on Tomkins's notion of shame, puts it: "Shame is the least toxic of the negative affects, for it operates in the context of positive affect and always carries the hope that the impeded good scene may return and, with it, the positive affect associated with it" (124). And so it is with Ismene's shame here, as this negative affect moves her to action (instead of depressing her into an inability to act), to repair the previous inaction that causes her to feel ashamed. It is this reparative effect of the affect of shame that orients Ismene, and *Antígona* as a text, towards the future and thus "conspires" to open spaces for new realities. Honig expresses this conspiratorial hope in this way (and I borrow her words to express my own hope):

> Conspiring with the canon, as it were, we let ourselves in on its secrets. We may find in it resources and energies that feed new politics and constitute new publics rather than just mirror, reconfirm, or resecure old states of affairs (…) conspiracy can press events to their illogical conclusions, thriving on their subtle rather than obvious implications, breaking their imperatives, and exploding their logics to open the way to what Arendt called "new relations and new realities." (*Antigone, Interrupted* 89)

I hope to have shown through this assemblage of close readings that the angles taken by *Antígona* with respect to *Antigone* and "Antigone" open political and affective spaces that are also spaces for the future, repairing, with the new actions of the characters, those actions as they have been told and read before. What we do in/with those spaces and feelings mobilized by the text, I cannot predict, nor intend to define. I have focused on the affects that the text mobilizes internally. But of course, the work will trigger feelings externally in its readers and spectators, and it is them (us) whom the text, if it is effective, ought to orient towards the future. Yet those feelings belong to the subjective sphere of aesthetic experience, and it is up to each reader, not to the critic, to give themselves to the event.[66]

Last corner: locality and postcoloniality

As a final meditation (or to use Derrida's still resonant metaphor, as an *envoi*) that touches more explicitly on some of the frames at work in this book, I want to turn once more to the question of whether we should always link the differences between the hypertext and the hypotext to the place where the former was written or, to use Fradinger's terminology, to the hypertext's "locality" ("Antígonas" 227). As I mentioned in the first part of this chapter, Fradinger argues against readings that compare Latin American Antígonas with their Greek precursor; rather, she proposes an analysis of dialogues between different versions internal to the region, in order to get "greater insights into [Antigone's] cultural history" ("Demanding the Political" 65). In contrast to this position stands, for instance, Emily Greenwood's notion of the text as "omni-local." In an illuminating example, Greenwood tells the anecdote of a teacher's experience of teaching Sophocles's *Antigone* alongside Griselda Gambaro's *Antígona furiosa* in a world literature class. The teacher remarked that "her students were struck by the gulf between critical responses to the two works: 'canonical works are often read, well, canonically, as articulating universals, as opposed to how their successors are often read and perhaps also taught–that is, as only local works'" ("Reception Studies" 43). At stake in the localizing move that struck the students in the anecdote is sustaining a hierarchy between, on the one hand, the "classic," canonical text with its alleged "universal" meaning, presumably unattached to a particular geography and time in history,[67] and, on the other hand, the modern version, understood as "local." To avoid reinstating that hierarchy and to trouble the notions of "universal" vs. "local," Greenwood proposes the concept of "omni-locality." The concept mobilizes the ancient text, signaling the geographical and cultural mobility that is already a part of the meanings of a canonical text, as they are historically construed. At the same time, it also signals that the reverse is true: that canonical texts were once also "local," and thus that locality is not a property of the successors ("Reception Studies" 43). Greenwood's concept is good in that it unsettles any presumed fixity and universality of the canonical text and thus avoids privileging the "original" source over its multiple and "ubiquitous but not universal" iterations, to put it with Erin Mee and Helene Foley (3). It is good also in that it reminds us that the geographical and cultural mobility that these ancient, canonical texts have enjoyed does not contradict the fact that they are also, in a sense, local texts. Mee and Foley argued similarly that "*if* there is anything 'universal' about Antigone, it lies in the way both the play and the character have been mobilized" (5, emphasis in the original). Yet, in order to avoid the problem of hyperlocalizing the successors of ancient texts, the concept of "omni-local" should also be applied to the recreations and adaptations of the canon. That is, coming back to the text that concerns us here, we need to also understand Watanabe's *Antígona* as (potentially) infinitely movable. This conceptual move is especially important when reading this version, as it purposely avoids localizing allusions and resists being read exclusively as a "Peruvianized" version of Sophocles, fixedly situated in the context of Peru's "Dirty War"—as it has been exclusively read.[68]

I am aware that one problem of trying to move away from localization and insisting, instead, on looking at the hypertextual relationship between *Antígona* and *Antigone* is the threat of what Catherine Holland calls "reinstating the past" (32). In order to avoid such reinstantiation, I have insisted on the ways in which *Antígona* is *unlike* Sophocles' *Antigone* but without situating those differences in the text's place and culture of origin. The difference I am interested in is not how the new text is "local," rather I am keen on looking at the textual (as opposed to the historically referential or allusive) means by which Watanabe's *Antígona* avoids "reinstating the past" that the ancient text carries with it. In my line of argumentation, this version avoids that reinstantiation not by localizing the plot of the story or the characters in modern-day Peru (there are no such obvious allusions) but rather by forgetting specific aspects of *Antigone* and "Antigone." As we saw, this hypertext forgets, among other things, precisely those aspects that would localize the play in its Greek religious, familiar, and ideological context. For instance, and to recapitulate, in this version, one does not come across Antigone's famous yet inscrutable justification for her decision, worthy of a brother but not a husband or child, to go against Creon's edict (Soph. *Ant.* 909–12)—a justification firmly rooted in the traditional role of women inside of the Ancient Greek aristocratic family.[69] Nor, I should add now, do we encounter her troubling (for a modern reader) claim that Polyneices deserves a burial because he is not a slave (Soph. *Ant.* 517)[70]—a claim deeply entrenched in the reality of fifth-century Athens. Also notably, there are no allusions to the family's incestuous history, which situates the Greek text within a broader web of ancient Greek myths, and has been the focus of so many interpretations. In this sense, *Antígona* does not reinstate the most culturally determined aspects of the Sophoclean version—which also happen to be the most politically backward, at least for a modern liberal or radical sensibility, to which I would posit this version is addressed.

And there is a second question that I want to corner in these closing remarks, which I have only treated implicitly up to now. It has to do with

Antígona's postcolonial status.[71] In taking a primarily "aesthetic" approach in my close reading of the text, I have not forgotten this important issue but rather have been responding to it from a different angle. My formal analysis is a way of considering the text's positionality with respect to the canon, that is, the politics of this text's take on the problem of imitation I gestured to at the beginning of this chapter. To restate my argument: this text freely intervenes into the hypertext and transforms its political and affective landscape, without addressing that transformation self-reflexively. Although the text was written and originally performed in a postcolonial context (or rather neocolonial),[72] it does not engage the canon with a criticism of its canonicity in mind. If it is critical of cultural hegemony, it is quietly so. Thus, concepts often used to describe the operations of postcolonial appropriations of canonical texts in general, and of Greek tragedy in particular, like "writing back"[73] or "canonical counter-discourse"[74] do not prove as helpful in trying to understand how the text positions itself vis-à-vis its imitative status.

I am also aware, of course, that the text's seeming disavowal of its postcolonial or neocolonial situation does not make the question irrelevant.[75] However, the question is further complicated by the fact that the experience of the classical texts in former colonies of Spain (as is the case with Peru) differs greatly from the experience of ex-British colonies, where the notions of "writing back to the empire" and "canonical counter-discourse" were developed.[76] Here is not the place to discuss those complexities at length, but three main problems complicating the use of the term "postcolonial" in the Latin American context are relevant and inescapable. First, the fact that most countries in Latin America (and Peru in particular) have been independent from Spain for over 200 years now, which raises the question of how much these cultures are determined by their prior colonial status; second, the fact that Latin American cultures are hybrids that underwent processes of creolization, making their relationship with Europe both external and internal (although this is not to say that there are no racial, political, and economic hierarchies sustained both during and after colonial times); and third, the fact that new forms of colonialism (neocolonialism) enforced by the United Sates (and first-world organizations like the International Monetary Fund) have come to occupy the position of the European ex-colonizers, as always, with the cooperation of local elites and perpetuated oppression. Because of these facts, in part unique to the region, scholars have addressed the specificities of the postcolonial and neocolonial context in Latin America and proposed concepts to think specifically about it.[77]

As mentioned before, thinking in particular about "Antigone" as it has been taken up in Latin America,[78] Moira Fradinger proposes the concept of *cannibalism* to describe the process whereby "Antigone" has been trans-culturized in the American continent for the past 200 years ("Demanding the Political" 63).[79] With the concept, as Andújar and Nikoloutsos note, she hints at "the legacy of the European classical as a matter somehow 'internal' to the region" rather than foreign" (*Greek and Romans* 7), at the same time that it renders visible the violent encounter with a foreign culture at the colonial origin of such legacy ("Demanding the Political" 63). And she also proposes the sibling concept of *rumination*, which in addition to the process of ingestion connotes "the obstinate memory" of this myth, signaling how "having ceased to be *external* to the Creole symbolic-digestive system, it returns from within the system to be re-created in the twentieth and twenty-first centuries" (64). Both Watanabe's and Ralli's *Antígona* participate in the ruminating process conceptualized by Fradinger, inserting themselves, as I already said, within those long chains of "obstinate memory" of the myth. They can certainly be interpreted in the theoretical assemblage proposed by Fradinger, who constructs a master narrative of Latin American (particularly South American) engagements with this myth as interventions in the continent's neocolonial history where the necro-political state has relied on the forced disappearance of bodies for the construction of neoliberal nations ("Demanding the Political"). My reluctance to do so is not that I think that such a reading would be wrong in the case of this particular *Antígona*—in fact, that is how it has mostly been read in the scholarship already. Rather, my reluctance to build on that narrative comes from a desire and need to render visible other multiple contextual and textual assemblages where *Antígona* makes meaning and gives pleasure, and also to see what it tells us when it is moved from its historical place, as the occasion of translation particularly invites us to do.

Yet, because the text aligns its own sympathies and those of its readers with the minoritarian and the dispossessed, as I argued above, I do think it does something along the lines of what Hardwick argues in other case studies of postcolonial writers (though not Latin American); Greek drama, she submits, has been used to "reveal the fragmentation of the ideologies of political and cultural oppression and have provided a commentary on different aspects of liberation from the colonization of the mind" ("Greek Drama" 241). Such decolonization of the mind, however, needs to be understood in the case of *Antígona*, not as liberation from the history of European imperialism, through which the Greek text came to form part of the "universal" canon, but rather from contemporary neocolonial realities that perpetrate forms of exclusion.

Thus, even more helpful, in my view, is Greenwood's Gramscian concept of "subaltern classics," which she develops in the context of African American and Anglophone-Caribbean engagements with classical texts. Greenwood proposes the term as an alternative in cases where the terms "postcolonial" and "anticolonial" do not fit as neatly. The term has the advantage of referring to different oppressed groups (e.g. slaves, peasants, religious minorities, women, different races and ethnic groups, the proletariat and the sub-proletariat), who "while their situations and degrees of empowerment will differ … have in common their restricted access to political representation and … self-representation in literature and history" ("Subaltern Classics" 578). I find Greenwood's "subaltern classic" fitting because, as I just said, this *Antígona* does align itself and its readers "in sympathy with the dispossessed" (580) (i.e. Antígona and Ismene), and it gives political representation to the voice of the minoritarian character of Ismene, thus also aligning itself, *avant la lettre*, with feminist turns towards the reparative possibilities of telling the myth from Ismene's perspective, as we also saw.

In my own approach, I have been intent on fleshing out *Antígona*'s intervention into its Greek source and its positionality with respect to part of the ancient myth's extensive histories of reception, considering the hypertext's subaltern positionality through an analysis of its affective and political landscapes. My close readings have been attuned to the text's complexity as a literary artifact, to its manifold desires and ways of giving pleasure by literary means. Using memory as a heuristic metaphor, extrapolating it from the text's own theme and form, I looked at literary operations through which it shapes loneliness and isolation as the affective texture of a failed political community and at the same time orients readers towards a future of peace and reparative care from within political failure.

Notes

1 I am blinking at Michael Cacoyannis' famous assertion that "a theatrical text is something of a paradox. It is written down, and yet it is not meant to be read" (*Euripides. The Bacchae* vii).
2 Hutcheon is thinking particularly about adaptations from books to film, but her conceptualization is still helpful to think about adaptation in general.
3 There is a vast field of memory studies from which, though aware, I am not borrowing the concept, for the field is built predominantly around memory understood culturally as opposed to literarily. Readers interested in this expansive and expanding area of studies and its possible links to literary memory can consult Pierre Nora's seminal work *Les lieux de memoir*, 1984. A good place to start is also *The Routledge International Handbook of Memory Studies*, 2015. For

a reading of Yuyachkani's *Antígona* as performance of cultural memory, see Diana Taylor "Staging Traumatic Memory" and Katherine Nigh. Here, I am concerned with memory exclusively as a hypertextual operation.

4 The difference between "strong" and "weak" theories is established by Tomkins in his seminal work *Affect, Imagery, Consciousness*. As Frank and Wilson summarize the distinction: "A strong theory is one that is able to account for large swaths of data and many eventualities. Psychoanalysis, especially in its classical Freudian forms, often makes use of strong theories (e.g., castration): it is able to engage, explain, and offer a conceptual infrastructure for a large archive of human behaviors, pleasures, fantasies, pathologies, and cultural productions. A weak theory, by contrast, has a much smaller compass. Its explanatory power is closely calibrated to the events at hand: a weak theory reads closely" (7). Sedgewick treats this especially in Chapter 4 of *Touching Feeling*.

5 I follow Worman in her use of *aisthesis* "in its most inclusive, embodied sense" (*Tragic Bodies* 6), which she has developed throughout her body of work, and see most recently "Touching Proximity," "Euripides," and *Tragic Bodies*.

6 As Sedgewick puts it: "What could better represent 'weak theory' (…) than the devalued and near obsolescent New Critical skill of imaginative close reading?" (145). I am not exactly following the New Critics, but my approach is certainly one of "imaginative close reading."

7 On the need to read with "strong" or "paranoid" theories along "weak" and "reparative" ones, see Heather Love.

8 I will come back to the issue of the postcoloniality of the text in the last section of this chapter.

9 Greenwood's work, as we will see in the last section of this chapter, counters such narratives specifically in the field of classical reception, looking at ways in which cases of subaltern receptions restitute the voice of the subaltern and recuperate its agency in Classical texts.

10 This question has already been addressed by other scholars. Most recently, Nikoloutsos and Gonçalves in the Introduction to a special dossier on classical receptions in Brazil argue for historical contextualization as a means to avoid uncritically ascribing to the ancient text the status of an "original": "Critical judgments of such modern responses must take into account an important component in the process whereby antiquity is recreated in modernity: the embeddedness of texts in their own time and over time, for writing and rewriting do not take place in a cultural vacuum. It is methodologically unorthodox to examine a given instance of reception only through comparison with the classical model precisely because the ancient source text is not the original. It is just another link in a long "chain of receptions" (See Jauss 1982: 20; Schmidt 1985: 70; Martindale 1993: 7 and 2007: 300) and incorporates previous (dominant or counter-hegemonic) interpretations and responses to the textual tradition from which it stems. Ancient texts are themselves rereadings of previous sources adapted to a specific cultural milieu" (14). See also Santiago, especially ch.2 and ch.4, pp. 60 ff. What does not seem to follow, from my perspective, is that in order to problematize the status of the ancient text as an "original," the only possible way of reading the new text is circumscribing it to a specific historical context. This assumed causality needs, in my opinion, to be more argued than it usually is, for it is not self-evident.

11 E.g. Martindale "Reception—A New Humanism?" and Hardwick "Aspirations and Mantras."

12 Another important influence, from within the field of classical reception, is Charles Martindale's seminal *Redeeming the Text*, which, also hinging heavily on postmodern and poststructuralist theory, is already concerned with the dismantling of the hierarchy between ancient and modern texts. If, as Martindale argues, the ancient text has come to mean (and accrue value) through its readings, then the value of the ancient "source" is of necessity relativized and that of its subsequent versions revaluated. The source of meaning, at least, is decentered, since, as Martindale puts it, texts "are endlessly *redescribable*. And they are constantly being made rereadable in multifarious ways, and in that sense are always 'in production'" (13). Most recently, Henao Castro borrows from art historian and affect theorist Mieke Bal the notion of "preposterous history" to think about *Antigone* as already always charged with the burden of its multiple historical readings. Henao Castro's original contribution is his proposition that the dominant, European readings of Antigone are possible only because of the colonization of the Americas—a connection thus far never made in the scholarship—further problematizing and destabilizing any presumed hierarchy (moral, political, aesthetic) between the ancient, canonical text and its subsequent *American* versions.

13 For a different reading of this opening line, although also focused on memory, see Lane "The Modernity of the Dead" 524ff.

14 Nigh takes a very different approach to the working of oblivion in the narrative created by memory, in relation to another work by Yuyachkani that also addresses Peru's Dirty War.

15 The scholarship on adaptations of Greek tragedy in general, and of Sophocles' *Antigone* in particular, is enormous. For a very recent study that covers the long history of adaptations, see Liapis and Sidiropoulou, Chanter and Kirkland, and Wilmer and Zukauskaite. For Antigone in Latin America, see specifically Henao Castro, Andújar and Nikoloutsos, Pianacci, and Fradinger.

16 For a discussion of different levels of readerly engagement, see Hardwick "Translating Greek plays" 338.

17 Focusing on Ralli's performance, and especially on the epitexts I discussed in the Introduction to this book, Jill Lane, for instance, whose reading is representative of the scholarly reception of *Antígona*, approached the problem of memory and the temporality of the play with the help of Benjamin's concept of a "dialectical image," which he defines as "that wherein what has been comes together in a flash with the now to form a constellation" (Benjamin, *Arcades* 462, qtd. in Lane, p. 526). According to Lane, "Ralli's sudden recognition of the women of Ayacucho as Antigone would be one thin filament of such a constellation, where the past of classical tragedy seems to burst into the present." From this view, her recognition—or ours—is not so much an insight into or an interpretation of the present, as it is a kind of unnamed memory. In sharing this memory with us, Ralli seems to take up the burden of the materialist historian as famously described by Benjamin: "to retain that image of the past which unexpectedly appears to man singled out by history at a moment of danger." (Lane 526) Memory, in Lane's reading, is historical memory: it is a memory of Antigone "bursting" in the present of the women of Ayacucho in Peru. Similar readings in this regard are Lambright; Martínez Tabares; Persino; and Robles Moreno. See also Cynthia Milton for a meditation on the role of art in generating historical memory in post-Shining Path Peru. Fradinger "Demanding the Political" also uses memory as a heuristic metaphor to analyse

Ariel Dorfman's version of Antigone, proposing the notion of a "memory of the political," but her focus is also on cultural history.

18 This is, of course, also the role of criticism, as some thinkers practice it. To put it with Bonnie Honig, whose work on Antigone I will engage later in this chapter and who proposes a way of approaching Sophocles' tragedy by, thinking with Walter Benjamin, "conspiring with the canon": "Benjamin presses on us throughout his work the idea that, like the messenger, we have both more and less agency than we think. We may be hopelessly embedded in structures and fantasies, discourses and iconographies, beyond our control but there is hope nonetheless. Small alterations, not always intended, may open up chasms of change—this is what Benjamin calls weak messianism" (Honig, *Antigone, Interrupted* 88).

19 McConnell suggests the concept of "sparagmos" to think of "creative artists' engagement with antiquity," particularly in postcolonial contexts. I find this concept productive in the cases that McConnell studies in her article, but I do not find the violence implied in the metaphor particularly suitable to what Watanabe's *Antígona* is doing.

20 I come back to this idea in the section "Hands-on narration: A reparative gesture."

21 ἀμήχανον δὲ παντὸς ἀνδρὸς ἐκμαθεῖν
    ψυχήν τε καὶ φρόνημα καὶ γνώμην, πρίν ἂν
    ἀρχαῖς τε καὶ νόμοισιν ἐντριβὴς φανῇι.

22 For a recent discussion of irony in Sophocles (although there is no treatment of this particular line), see Goldhill, especially Chapter 1.

23 For a slightly different reading of this resignation, see Cancela Miranada 25.

24 Technically, this is the third intervention of the chorus, yet the convention is to mark the first appearance of the chorus (*parodos*) as different and to start counting its other passages (*stasima*) from the second on. Thus, the choral passage that appears secondly is termed the "first *stasimon*" and so on.

25 It should be noted that "peace" also appears as something to celebrate in Gambaro's *Antígona furiosa*, p. 200.

26 As opposed to, for example, the desire for death associated with Antigone since Lacan's influential interpretation. Lacan famously reads Antigone as a character that "pushes to the limit the realization of something that might be called the pure and simple desire of death as such. She incarnates that desire" (Lacan 282). For recent discussions of Lacan's reading, see the Introduction and Chapters 5, 6 and 8 in S. E. Wilmer and Audrone Zukauskaite.

27 Soph. *Ant.* 332–83. The adjective Sophocles uses here *deinós* is particularly polyvalent. As Mark Griffith comments in the ad hoc note in his edition of the tragedy, "here it soon becomes obvious that the epithet has been chosen precisely because of its multivalence ('terrible', 'awe-inspiring', 'wonderful', 'strange', 'clever', 'extraordinary')." For a close reading of this stasimon, focused on its take on temporality, see Kirkland 56–60.

28 πολλὰ τὰ δεινὰ κοὐδὲν ἀν-
    θρώπου δεινότερον πέλει

29 Soph. *Ant.* 361. Translations of Sophocles are mine here and elsewhere.

30 For a reading that focuses on the role of the body in Sophocles' *Antigone*, the reader may go to Adriana Cavarero's chapter "On the Body of Antigone" in Fanny Söderbäck.

31 Surprisingly, this line in Watanabe recalls a poem by George Seferis, which casts Euripides' vision of human veins as 'a net the gods made to trap us in like wild beasts'" (quoted by Worman, *Tragic Bodies* 16).

32 Chanter notes that, in Sophocles, Antigone's encounter with her brother's corpse causes her to become "monstrous" (the sounds she makes are compared to those of birds), as the character has often been read by critics since Heidegger. Chanter problematizes those readings and says: "Rather than quickly resolving the unreadability of Antigone's metamorphosis into monstrosity, the abject cause of that monstrosity needs to be borne in mind: Polyneices' decomposing body" (37).

33 For a discussion of this ambiguity, see Cairns *ad loc.*

34 It should be noted that eroding the tragedy's sympathy away from Creonte and closer to Antígona is something that this version shares in common with many modern versions of the Greek tragedy. Twentieth-century writers engaging with the ancient myth have been mostly concerned with the righteousness of Antigone's character. Because the tragedy has often been re-written to address oppressive historical events (in Latin America and around the world), there is seldom an interest in exploring the nuances of the position of someone in power, and modern audiences are almost never asked to sympathize with Creon. For example, staying only with some of the best-known versions in Latin America and the Caribbean (more case studies out of Latin America and Europe can be found in Mee and Foley): Feliks Morisseau-Leroy's *Antigòn* is so tyrannical he even calls on the spirits to come and stab Antigòn's soul ("You see that I am right. I stab Antigòn's soul," qtd. in Hawkins 190–1; see also Fradinger "Danbala's Daughters"); in Griselda Gambaro's *Antígona furiosa* (1986)—mentioned in the Introduction—Creonte is not even a character but only a textual source who is quoted and then parodically embodied by one of the characters; more recently, in Perla de la Rosa's *Antígona: las voces que incendian el desierto* (2004), Creonte is assimilated to the state complicit in the massive feminicides (see Weiner).

35 The lines are so difficult to make sense of that commentators since Jebb (1902) has wanted to excise them, thinking them "unworthy" of Sophocles. See Goldhill 245.

36 On experimentations with genre in contemporary adaptations of Greek tragedy, see Foley "Generic Ambiguity."

37 I use this term in a restricted sense only to point out that the monologues have qualities we usually associate with lyric poetry (Watanabe's poetry, to begin with), but I do not mean to align Watanabe's monologues with the much more technical use of the term "dramatic monologue," usually associated with the lyric poetry of Alfred Tennyson and Robert Browning.

38 The literary device "monologue" is defined in the *Princeton Encyclopedia of Poetry and Poetics* thus: "in the widest sense, a sustained first person utterance for which, whether or not an audience is expressly evoked, rhetorical motives outweigh meditative or deliberative ones." Lyric poems can often be considered monologues in this broad sense. A "soliloquy," a kind of monologue, is defined as "a form of monologue in which an actor speaks alone on stage." For convenience, I prefer to use "monologue" over the stricter definition of "soliloquy," as it allows for a more nuanced analysis of what the text is doing with this device.

The spectator who sees Ralli's original performance of the text, in which she alone interprets all the characters, also faces the strangeness of this world where everyone talks to themselves—and of course, as we saw in the Introduction, this is one way in which the actress left traces on the form of the written text.

39 Genette calls this "redistribution of what is shown and what is left out" (*Palimpsests* 285). He looks at this modal device in the context of intermodal transformation, but it applies here as well.

40 Hardwick suggests a similar reading, but where I am interested in the creases of the texts, Hardwick looks at how these "repressions" (sic) "expose faultlines and shifts in the tectonics of cultural capital" ("Thinking with Classical Reception" 19–20).

41 This is already observable in antiquity, as ancient playwrights usually reworked versions of the myths, fleshing out new aspects that were before obscure or bringing new threads into the plots.

42 Castagno notes: "In reality-based drama, monologue may theatricalize what Dorrit Cohn has described as the transparent mind, allowing audiences entry into the characters' consciousness: their motivations, history, or point of view. As Cohn posits, 'If the real world becomes fiction only by revealing the hidden side of human beings, the reverse is equally true: the most real, the 'roundest' characters of fiction are those we know most intimately, precisely in ways we could never know people in real life' (1978, 5). This psychological 'rounding' provided by monologue serves to texture the dramatized action. The Aristotelian action expands to include the articulation of thought processes, emotional states, visual metaphors, and so on" (139). Although I do not consider *Antígona* "reality-based drama," I think Castagno's observations about the monologue still apply.

43 In "Fragments" and *El desmontaje*, Ralli specifically mentions this quality with which Antigone is often characterized (she even mentions Griselda Gambaro's *Antígona Furiosa*) as something her performance challenged, giving to her Antígona a more apparently fragile demeanor, much like the demeanor she observed in the Peruvian women she interviewed during her research. Perhaps this marks another way in which the work of the actress intertwines with the texture of the text.

44 For instance, as Honig notes, Antigone's reasoning for burying Polyneices, alleging his irreplaceability (Soph. *Ant.* 909–12), has gained her some enemies over the centuries, some of whom have been so repelled that they have even argued that the passage must be inauthentic. See *Antigone, Interrupted* 123.

45 See *Antigone* 876–882: ἄκλαυτος (without fame), ἄφιλος (friendless), ἀνυμέναιος (unwed); 916–920: ἄλεκτρον (virgin), ἀνυμέναιον (unwed), ἐρῆμος πρὸς φίλων (deprived of friends).

46 This isolation and loneliness that comes from the monologues is a result of the collaborative process with Teresa Ralli, as it was the restriction imposed upon the poet by the actress that the production would be a one woman performance the choice to have monologues instead of dialogues. Yet, the poetic effects of this choice far surpass the original circumstances that gave occasion to it.

47 As noted by Miranda Cancela, this line reworks lines 879–80 of Sophocles' *Antigone* (26). As Martínez Tabares also notes, Watanabe talks about the image of dissolving into the light as something that he did not take from Sophocles, but as a personal concern that he interwove with the Sophoclean hypotext: "There was a need to delineate Antígona's character. I added these poem-monologues using my own concerns, what in Peru we call *paltas*—my own internal conflicts embodied in Antígona, like dying, trying to dissolve into light, dying without going through the physical fact of death, as Antígona

says "maybe to dissolve into the light." I had to create those scenes in order to give more weight to Antígona, with the result that she is shut in there, alone, reflecting, with words of Sophocles and of mine" (my translation). According to this narrative, Watanabe uses a personal obsession—much of his poetry is in fact concerned with the bodilyness of the body and the experience of death—to "give more weight" to the character of Antígona. He uses the form of the monologue and themes of his own poetic concern to intervene the Sophoclean model and produce a heroine that is, in his words, "shut in there, alone, reflecting, with words of Sophocles and of mine." Yet, by tracing this horizontal axis with respect to the vertical axis of the structural analysis, I am looking at an epitext (the interview) and inscribing the topic of solitude onto Watanabe's body, his lived experiences, and obsessions. These biographical details are relevant to a formal analysis in as much as they expand the places of pleasure we can experience in our study of the text, if not necessarily its meaning. And taking them into account goes only as far as saying that a writer brings himself with him when he sits down to write. More interesting is perhaps to single out the convergence that Watanabe mentions: "with words of Sophocles and of mine." For, in fact, the body plays a central role in Sophocles' *Antigone*, only in ways that are rather different from Watanabe's.

48 Bonnie Honig argues that the Creon of the Sophoclean tragedy conforms to fifth-century Athens democratic norms, and that, through the figures of Antigone and Creon, Sophocles "stages encounters between Homeric and classical mourning practices cast as excessive or well-judged" ("Antigone's Lament" 13).

49 Lehman identifies plot as a characteristic of dramatic theater, which he opposes to "postdramatic." For instance, in the Prologue he says: "Theatre is tacitly thought of as the *theatre of dramas*. Among its consciously theorized elements are the categories of 'imitation' and 'action'/'plot', as much as the virtually automatic intimate connection of the two. As an associated, rather unconscious motif of this classical theatre conception we can point out the attempt to form (or strengthen) a social bond through theatre, a community uniting the audience and the stage emotionally and mentally. 'Catharsis' is the displaced theoretical name for this – by no means primarily aesthetic – function of theatre" (21) He also identifies "suspense" as one of drama's "ingredients": "With the criterion 'suspense' the classical understanding of drama, or more precisely a certain ingredient of it, lives on. Exposition, ascending action, peripeteia and catastrophe: as old-fashioned as it may sound, these are what people expect of an entertaining story in film and theatre" (24). In the section named "Suspended Suspense," Lehman argues that the idea of "suspense" sustains traditional notions of theater as drama: "With the criterion 'suspense' the classical understanding of drama, or more precisely a certain ingredient of it, lives on. Exposition, ascending action, peripeteia and catastrophe: as old-fashioned as it may sound, these are what people expect of an entertaining story in film and theatre" (34).

50 See Cole; also Campbell "Medea Material" and "Postdramatic Greek Tragedies."

51 On postdramatic theater's fragmentary and anti-representation aesthetics, see Lehman 22, 37, 82–3, 85–7, and 127. I think it is safer to frame the use of the monologue and narration in *Antígona*, on the one hand, within the European poetic tradition of the dramatic monologue, with which Watanabe's use of

the monologue shares certain characteristics, and on the other hand, within Brechtian poetics—as opposed to postdramatic, which Lehman defines as post-Brechtian. (Though Cole argues that many postdramatic productions are not as decisively post-Brechtian as Lehman would have it, see Cole 6. For the importance of Brecht in Latin American theater in general, see Brunn 36–47.) Here is not the place to review the tradition of the dramatic monologue, and I leave it to the interested reader to pursue further research on the topic. About Brecht, however, it is important to say at least that his poetics of Epic Theater famously reintroduced the use of narration specifically as a distancing device (i.e. to make the familiar appear strange). Brecht positioned his theater directly against an Aristotelian poetics, dominant since the Renaissance. Yet despite Brecht's important ruptures with conventional drama, Lehman considers him at the threshold of the postdramatic, because, in his view, Brecht's Epic Theater retained a number of Aristotelian features, "including the conventional dramatic form of the scripts and the traditional ideas of plot and character to which they adhere" (Cole 5). Watanabe's use of a Narradora that remembers the events of the plot certainly creates a certain Brechtian distancing effect, hinting at the very role of memory and the act of remembering and memorializing as such. At the same time, Watanabe maintains the centrality of plot and character, for even though the structure of the text in a sequence of monologues is quite fragmentary, discontinuities are not emphasized, and the experience of reading is not disorienting in terms of time and the connections between actions and characters.

52 A production of Watanabe's text staged in Mexico City in 2005, directed by Miguel Ángel Rivera, is described in a newspaper review as "a symphonic poem" (*Revista Tiempo Libre*, December 1, 2005, p.25). For a brief note on this production, see the Appendix to this book.

53 For a meditation on postmodern irony, inflected by nostaligia, see Hutcheon "Irony, Nostalgia, and the Postmodern: A Dialogue."

54 See Lyotard.

55 Hardwick proposes a model for the process of political engagement that Greek tragedy experienced in the late 1960s in Europe and the United States. She argues that Greek tragedy emancipated itself from closed appropriation or association with any one class or ideology; achieved civic participation in new contexts; and created space in which to develop politically and culturally. Although Hardwick is not talking about Latin America, Watanabe's and Yuyachkani's *Antígona* (both the text and the performance) fit within that model. See Hardwick "Greek Drama and Anticolonialism."

56 For the most recent reassessment of this interpretation, see Moro.

57 For synesthesia in antiquity, though not focused on ancient tragedy, see Butler and Purves.

58 I borrow the idea from Moro, who interprets the relationship between Antigone and Ismene in Sophocles' *Antigone* as a collaborative one, even if agonistically so. In the process of mutual confrontation motivated by mutual care for each other's lives, Moro argues, the two enact the process of "becoming sisters" (123).

59 For hands and touch in the tragedies around Oedipus' family, see ch. 1 in Worman, *Tragic Bodies*.

60 Errandonea's Spanish rendition (on which Watanabe based his version) preserves the mention of the hands in the Greek: "¿Quieres ayudar a estas manos a levantar aquel cadáver?" (92).

61 I am borrowing these notions from Hutcheon *A Poetics* 12.

62 Recent scholarship has turned its attention to the dynamics of sisterhood in *Antigone* (and in Sophocles in general). As a result, the character of Ismene has been rescued from the shadows of criticism and emerged as a central figure of analysis. In addition to Honig "Ismene's Forced Choice" and Rawlinson "Beyond Antigone" and "Antigone and Ismene," see, e.g. Butler *Antigone's Claim*; Englelstein; Roisman; Moro, and Coo "Greek Tragedy." On the creative side, e.g. Colm Tóibín's *Pale Sister*, is a version of Antigone that also centers on the character of Ismene. Like Watanabe, Tóibín wrote his piece specifically for an actress, Lisa Dwan; it was first presented and published in 2019. In 2004, Miyagi Satoshi directed an *Antigone* in Japan that also identifies Ismene with the citizens that witnessed and (complicitly) survived a catastrophe, in that case World War II (see Smethurst).

63 As Lyndsay Coo notes, the pairing of a weaker and a stronger sister is also present in Sophocles' *Electra*, and "this portrait of two contrasting sisters has been recognised since antiquity as distinctively Sophoclean" ("Shifting Sisterhood" 89) As Coo also notes, the trend of comparing Electra/Chrysothemis to Antigone/Ismene goes back to the ancient scholia (Σ Soph. *El.* 328, pp. 162f. Xenis). For the assimilation of Ismene and Chrysothemis already in the early fourth century BC, see Coo "A Sophoclean Slip."

64 See note 62. For a critical perspective on Honig's and other feminist readings, see Goldhill, ch. 9.

65 Cf. Fischer-Lichte's analysis of guilt in productions of *Oedipus the King* in postwar Germany.

66 For a lucid attempt to think about affects as an experience of the viewer (spectator, reader, etc.) of a work of art, see Bal.

67 Though of course a long list of scholars have worked to historicize these texts.

68 See footnote 34 and the Introduction to this book.

69 See Foley *The Conception of Women* 129–31. Judith Butler's discussion of this passage and of Antigone's "law" represents an important turning point in interpretations of the myth and figure of Antigone, seminal especially for queer readings of the play, for which see Butler 9ff.

70 There is an entire tradition of receptions of Antigone in the Global South that focuses precisely on this claim. See Henao Castro 6.

71 For an excellent introduction to the main concepts and problems of postcolonial theory, the interested reader can read Annia Loomba, *Colonialism/ Postcolonialism*.

72 For the problems of the concept of postcolonialism in the Americas, see e.g. Goff and Simpson; Andújar and Nikoloutsos; and Henao Castro. A good introduction to key concepts of postcolonial studies is Steinmeyer.

73 The idea was originally formulated by Salman Rushdie and was taken up in literary studies by Ashcroft et al. Greenwood still uses the notion of writing back in her analysis of what she calls "subaltern classics" (see "Subaltern Classics" 579).

74 The notion is proposed by Tiffin, who defines it thus: "This strategy … is one in which a post-colonial writer takes up a character or characters, or the basic assumptions of a British canonical text, and unveils those assumptions, subverting the text for post-colonial purposes" (97). Hardwick takes a similar approach, when she looks at classical plays used as "counter-texts" or "basis for critique and intervention" in British postcolonial contexts (see "Refiguring Classical Texts").

75 Young's remark about the continuous relevance of postcolonial theory seems fitting: "'Postcolonialism' is not just a disciplinary field, nor is it a theory which has or has not come to an end. Rather, its objectives have always involved a wide-ranging political project—to reconstruct Western knowledge formations, reorient ethical norms, turn the power structures of the world upside down, refashion the world from below. The postcolonial has always been concerned with interrogating the interrelated histories of violence, domination, inequality, and injustice, with addressing the fact that, and the reasons why, millions of people in this world still live without things that most of those in the West take for granted. Clean water, for example" (20).

76 For a succinct exposition of the state of the issue, see Andújar and Nikoloutsos 1–5.

77 See e.g. Klor de Alva; Mignolo; Hulme; Coronil; and Moraña et al. Gilbert Shang Ndi' literary analysis of the historical foundations of violence in colonial Peru can also be of interest.

78 What is called "Latin America" is not a continent but a vast region including most of the hemisphere down from the southern border of the United States and Mexico. Mexico, Central America, the Spanish-speaking Caribbean, Brazil, and the Southern Cone are all distinct regions with their own regional histories that are hardly encompassed under the generalizing term "Latin America." (For a brief but helpful discussion of the term with further references, see Andújar and Nikoloutsos 2ff.) However, the term is handy because, despite the diversity of local histories, the countries in this vast region share important elements in common, such as overlapping histories of colonization by the Spanish and Portuguese empires that came to an "end" with independence wars in the nineteenth century—with the exception of Puerto Rico, which passed directly from Spain into the dominion of the United States and never achieved independence, but is still a Spanish-speaking territory and very much "Hispanic" in cultural terms. The region also shares the hybrid nature of their individual cultures, which in most cases include Native Indian and African cultures mixed with, while violently subdued by, the Europeans;, in postcolonial times, the neocolonial subjection to the United States, which in many of the countries resulted in US-backed dictatorships to subdue land redistribution, socialist and communist movements (from the 1950s through to the 1990s), imposed austerity measures and trade agreements, a massive drug market, and subsequent waves of migrations due to the resultant violence and impoverishment. Henao Castro thinks of this shared reality in terms of "settler-colonial capitalism produced through the European conquest of the Americas" (4; for his development of this concept and his lucid and ground-breaking claim that it already informs our readings of *Antigone*, see his whole Introduction).

79 See also Fradinger "An Argentine Tradition" and "Danbala's Daughters."

Works cited

Alonso, Laura. "La Narración Como Situación Enunciativa y el Predominio del 'Ethos' en *Antígona* de José Watanabe y el Grupo Yuyachkani." *Latin American Theatre Review*, vol. 44, no. 2, 2011, pp. 55–67.

Andújar, Rosa, and Konstantinos Nikoloutsos, editors. *Greeks and Romans on the Latin American Stage*. Bloomsbury Academic, 2020, https://2020, 10.5040/9781350125643.

Aschcroft, Bill et al., editors. *The Empire Writes Back: Theory and Practices in Postcolonial Literatures*. E-book, 2nd ed., Routledge, 2002.

Bal, Mieke. "Affectively Effective: Affect as an Artistic-Political Strategy." *How to Do Things with Affects: Affective Triggers in Aesthetic Forms and Cultural Practices*, edited by Ernst van Alphen and Tomáš Jirsa, E-book, Brill, 2019, pp. 179–99.

Brinkema, Eugenie. *The Forms of the Affects*. Duke University Press, 2014, https://doi-org.ezproxy.cul.columbia.edu/10.1215/9780822376774.

Brunn, Victoria. "Revolutionizing *Antigone*: A Puerto Rican Adaptation of Sophocles' Tragedy." *Romance Quarterly*, vol. 59, no. 1, 2012, pp. 36–47.

Burgin, Victor. *The End of Art Theory: Criticism and Postmodernity*. New Jersey, Humanities Press International, 1986.

Butler, Judith. *Antigone's Claim: Kinship between Life and Death*. E-book, Columbia University Press, 2000.

Butler, Sean and Alex Purves, editors. *Synaesthesia and the Ancient Senses*. Routledge, 2013, https://doi-org.ezproxy.cul.columbia.edu/10.4324/9781315729848.

Cacoyannis, Michael, translator. *Euripides. The Bacchae*. Meridian/Penguin, 1987.

Cairns, Douglas. *Sophocles: Antigone*. Bloomsbury Academic, 2016.

Campbell, Patrick. "Medea Material: Heiner Müller, Myth, and Text." *Modern Drama*, vol. 51, no. 1, pp. 84–103.

———. "Postdramatic Greek Tragedies." *Journal of Dramatic Theory and Criticism*, vol. 25, no. 1, 2010, pp. 55–74.

Carson, Anne. *Economy of the Unlost*. Princeton University Press, 1999.

Castagno, Paul. *New Playwriting Strategies: A Language Based Approach to Playwriting*. Routledge, 2001, https://doi-org.ezproxy.cul.columbia.edu/10.4324/97813150 59808.

Chanter, Tina. "Antigone's Political Legacies: Abjection in Defiance of Mourning." Wilmer and Zukauskaité, pp. 19–47.

Chanter, Tina and Sean D. Kirkland, editors. *The Returns of Antígona: Interdisciplinary Essays*. SUNY Press, 2014.

Cole, Emma. *Postdramatic Tragedies*. Oxford, Oxford University Press, 2019, https://oxford-universitypressscholarship-com.ezproxy.cul.columbia.edu/view/10.1093/oso/9780198817680.001.0001/oso-9780198817680.

Coo, Lyndsay. "A Sophoclean Slip: Mistaken Identity and Tragic Allusion on the Exeter Pelike." *Bulletin of the Institute of Classical Studies*, vol. 56, pp. 67–88.

———. "Shifting Sisterhood: Electra and Chrysothemis in Sophocles' *Electra*." In Terms of Athens, special issue of *Ramus*, vol. 50, nos. 1–2, 2021, pp. 89–108.

Derrida, Jacques. "Signature Event Contextt." *Margins of Philosophy*, by Jacques Derrida. Translated by Alan Bass, The University of Chicago Press, 1982.

Engelstein, Stefani. "Sibling Logic; or, Antigone Again." *Publications of the Modern Language Association of America*, vol. 1, no.1, 2011, pp. 38–54.

———. "Ismene on Horseback and Other Subjects." *Philosophy Today*, vol. 59, no. 3, 2015, pp. 562–5.

Errandonea, Ignacio. "Antígona." *La Tragedia Griega*, edited by Pedro E. Badillo, Universidad de Puerto Rico, 2004.

Fischer-Lichte, Erika. *Tragedy's Endurance: Performances of Greek Tragedies and Cultural Identity in Germany since 1800*. Oxford University Press, 2017, https://oxforduniversitypressscholarship-com.ezproxy.cul.columbia.edu/view/10.1093/oso/9780199651634.001.0001/oso-9780199651634.

Foley, Helene. *The Conception of Women in Athenian Drama*. Routledge, 1981.

———. "Generic Ambiguity in Modern Productions and New Versions of Greek Tragedy," Hall and Harrop, 2010, pp. 137–52.

Fradinger, Moira. "An Argentine Tradition." Mee and Foley, pp. 67–89.

———. "Danbala's Daughter: Félix Morisseau-Leroy's *Antigòn an Kreyòl*," Mee and Foley, pp. 127–46.

———. "Demanding the Political: *Widows*, or Ariel Dorfman's Antigones." *Whose Voice is This? Iberian and Latin American Antigones*, special issue of *Hispanic Issues on Line*, edited by Jennifer Duprey, vol. 13, 2013, pp. 63–81.

———. "Antígonas: On the Uses of Tragedy." Chanter and Kirkland, pp. 223–39.

Frank, Adam and Elizabeth Wilson, editors. *A Silvan Tomkins Handbook: Foundations for Affect Theory*. University of Minnesota Press, 2020, https://muse.jhu.edu/book/78624.

Gambaro, Griselda. *Information for Foreigners: Three Plays*. Translated by Marguerite Feitlowitz, Northwestern University Press, 1992.

Genette, Gerard. *Paratexts: Thresholds of Interpretation*. Translated by Jane E. Lewin, E-book, Cambridge University Press, 1997.

———. *Palimpsests: Literature in the Second Degree*. Translated by Channa Newman and Claude Doubinsky, University of Nebraska Press: Lincoln, Nebraska, 1997, https://hdl-handle-net.ezproxy.cul.columbia.edu/2027/heb.09358.

Goldhill, Simon. *Sophocles and the Language of Tragedy*. Oxford University Press, 2012, https:/ 10.1093/acprof:oso/9780199796274.001.0001.

Goff, Barbara and Michael Simpson. "New Worlds, Old Dreams?: Postcolonial Theory and Reception of Greek Drama." Katherine Bosher et al., editors, *The Oxford Handbook of Greek Drama in the Americas*, Oxford University Press, 2015, pp. 29–51, https://10.1093/oxfordhb/9780199661305.001.0001.

Greenwood, Emily. "Reception Studies: The Cultural Mobility of Classics." *Daedalus*, vol. 145, no. 2, 2016, pp. 41–9.

———. "Subaltern Classics in Anti- and Post-Colonial Literatures in English." *The Oxford History of Classical Reception in English Literature*, edited by Kenneth Haynes, vol. 5, Oxford University Press, 2019, pp. 576–607, https://10.1093/acprof:oso/9780199587230.001.0001.

Griffith, Mark. *Sophocles. Antigone*. Cambridge University Press, 1999.

Hardwick, Lorna. "Greek Drama and Anti-Colonialism: Decolonizing Classics." *Dionysus Since 69: Greek Tragedy at the Dawn of the Third Millennium*, edited by Edith Hall et al., e-book, Oxford University Press, 2004, pp. 219–42.

———. "Refiguring Classical Texts." *Classics and Colonialism*, edited by Barbara Goff, Duckworth, 2005, pp. 107–17.

———. "Fuzzy Connections. Classical Texts and Modern Poetry in English." *Tradition, Translation, Trauma: The Classic and the Modern*, edited by Jan Parker and Timothy Mathews, e-book, Oxford University Press, 2011, pp. 39–60.

————. "Translating Greek Plays for Theatre Today: Transmission, Transgression, Transformation." *Target. International Journal of Translation Studies*, vol. 25, no. 3, 2013, pp. 321–42.

————. "Thinking with Classical Reception: Critical Distance, Critical Licence, Critical Amnesia?" *Classics in extremis: The Edges of Classical Reception*, edited by Edmund Richardson Bloomsbury, 2019, pp. 13–24.

————. "Aspirations and Mantras in Classical Reception Research: Can There Really be a Dialogue between Ancient and Modern?" *Framing Classical Reception Studies: Different Perspectives on a Developing Field*, edited by Maarten De Pourcq et al., e-book, Brill, 2020.

Hardwick, Lorna and Carol Gillespie. Introduction. *Classics in Post-Colonial Worlds*. E-book, Oxford University Press, 2007, pp. 1–12, https://oxford-universitypressscholarship-com.ezproxy.cul.columbia.edu/view/10.1093/acprof:oso/9780199296101.001.0001/acprof-9780199296101.

Hawkins, Tom. "Dismantling the Anthropological Machine: Feliks Moriso-Lewa's *Antigòn* and Luis Alfaro's *Electricidad*." Andújar and Nikoloutsos, pp. 185–98.

Holland, Catherine. "After Antigone: Women, the Past and the Present of Feminist Political Thought." Söderback, pp. 27–43.

Honig, Bonnie. "Antigone's Laments, Creon's Grief: Mourning, Membership, and the Politics of Exception." *Political Theory*, vol. 37, no. 1, pp. 5–43.

————. "Ismene's Forced Choice: Sacrifice and Sorority in Sophocles' *Antigone*." *Arethusa*, vol. 44, no. 1, 2011, pp. 29–68.

————. *Antigone, Interrupted*. E-book, Cambridge University Press, 2013.

Hulme, Peter. "Postcolonial Theory and the Representation of Culture in the Americas." *Coloniality at Large: Latin America and the Postcolonial Debate*, edited by Manuel Moraña et al., Duke University Press, 2008, pp. 388–95.

Hutcheon, Linda. *A Poetics of Postmodernism: History, Theory, Fiction*. E-book, Routledge, 1988.

————. "Irony, Nostalgia, and the Postmodern: A Dialogue." *Poligrafías: Revista de Teoría Literaria y Literatura Comparada*, no. 3, 1998, pp. 18–41.

————. *A Theory of Adaptation*. E-book, Routledge, 2012.

Kirkland, Sean D. "Tragic Time." Chanter and Kirkland, pp. 51–67.

Klor de Alva, José. "The Postcolonization of the (Latin) American Experience: A Reconsideration of 'Colonialism,' 'Postcolonialism,' and 'Mestizaje'". *After Colonialism: Imperial Histories and Postcolonial Displacements*, edited by Gyan Prakash, e-book, Princeton University Press, 1995, pp. 241–76.

Lacan, Jacques. *The Seminar of Jacques Lacan: The Ethics of Psychoanalysis Book VII, 1959– 1960*. W.W. Norton and Routledge, 1992.

Lane, Jill. "*Antígona* and the Modernity of the Dead." *Modern Drama*, vol. 50, no. 4, 2007, pp. 517–31.

Lambright, Anne. "Woman, Body and Memory: Yuyachkani's Peruvian Antígone." *Feminist Scholarship Review*, vol. XI, no. 1, 2001, pp. 7–11.

Lehman, Hans-Georg. *Postdramatic Theatre*. Translated by Karen Jürs-Munby. E-book, London, Routledge, 2006, https://doi-org.ezproxy.cul.columbia.edu/10.4324/9780203088104.

Liapis Vayos, and Avra Sidiriopoulou, editors. *Adapting Greek Tragedy: Contemporary Contexts for Ancient Texts*. Cambridge University Press, 2021, https://doi-org.ezproxy.cul.columbia.edu/10.1017/9781316659168.

Loomba, Ania. *Colonialism/Postcolonialism*. E-book, Routledge, 1998.

Love, Heather. "Truth and Consequences: On Paranoid Reading and Reparative Reading." *Criticism*, vol. 52, no. 2, 2010, pp. 235–41.

Lyotard, Jean Francois. *The Postmodern Condition: A Report on Knowledge.* University of Minnesota Press, 1984.

Martínez Tabares, Vivian. "Despertar la Memoria y el Gesto de Ismene." *Revista Conjunto*, vol. 121, 2001, pp. 10–6.

Martindale, Charles. *Redeeming the Text: Latin Poetry and the Hermeneutics of Reception.* Cambridge University Press, 1993.

———. "Reception—A New Humanism? Receptivity, Pedagogy, the Transhistorical." *Classical Receptions Journal*, vol. 5, no. 2, 2013, pp. 169–83.

———. "Thinking Through Reception." *Classics and the Uses of Reception*, edited by Charles Martindale and Richard Thomas, e-book, Blackwell, 2006, pp. 1–13.

Mee, Ericn, and Helene Foley, editors. *Antigone on the Contemporary World Stage.* Oxford University Press, 2011, https://oxford-universitypressscholarship-com. ezproxy.cul.columbia.edu/view/10.1093/acprof:oso/9780199586196. 001.0001/acpro f-9780199586196.

Meineck, Peter. "Forsaking the Fidelity Discourse: The Application of Adaptation." Liapis and Sidiropoulou, pp. 77–109, https://doi.org/10.1017/9781316659168.006.

Milton, Cynthia, editor. *Art from a Fractured Past: Memory and Truth Telling in Post-Shining Path's Peru.* Duke University Press, 2014, https://muse.jhu.edu/book/64012 ER.

Mignolo, Walter. *Local Histories/Global Designs: Coloniality, Subaltern Knowledges, and Border Thinking.* Princeton University Press, 2000, https://www-jstor-org. ezproxy.cul.columbia.edu/stable/j.ctt7s237.

Moro, Valentina. "Sailing Together: The Agonistic Construction of Sisterhood in Sophocles' *Antigone.*" *In Terms of Athens*, special issue of *Ramus*, vol. 50, nos.1–2, 2021, pp. 109–26.

Nathanson, Donald. "Shame and the Affect Theory of Silvan Tomkins." *The Widening Scope of Shame*, edited by Melvin R. Lansky and Andrew P. Morris, 1998, pp. 107–38, https://doi-org.ezproxy.cul.columbia.edu/10.4324/9781315803388.

Ndi, Gilbert Shang. *Memories of Violence in Peru and the Congo: Writing on the Brink.* Routledge, 2022, https://doi-org.ezproxy.cul.columbia.edu/10.4324/9781003158202.

Nikoloutsos, Konstantinos, and Rodrigo Tadeu Gonçalves. "Classical Tradition in Brazil: Translation, Rewriting, and Reception." *Caletroscópio*, vol. 6, no. 1, 2018, pp. 11–20.

Ousby, Ian, editor. *The Cambridge Guide to Literature in English.* E-book, Cambridge University Press, 1988.

Persino, María Silvina. "Cuerpo y Memoria en el Teatro de Los Andes y Yuyachkani." *Gestos*, vol. 22, no. 43, 2007, pp. 87–103.

Pianacci, Rómulo. *Antígona: Una Tragedia Latinoamericana.* Buenos Aires, Losada, 2015.

Purves, Alex, editor. *Touch and the Ancient Senses.* Routledge, 2018, https://doi-org.ezproxy.cul.columbia.edu/10.4324/9781315719665.

Ralli, Teresa. "Fragments of Memory." Translated by Margaret Carson, Taylor and Constantino, pp. 355–64.

Rawlinson, Mary C. "Beyond Antigone: Ismene, Gender, and the Right to Life." Chanter and Kirkland, pp. 101–22.

———. "Antigone and Ismene: Hard Heads, Hard Hearts, and the Claim of the Right." *Just Life: Bioethics and the Future of Sexual Difference*. E-book, Columbia University Press, 2016, pp. 83–105.

Robles Moreno, Leticia. "Yo Soy la Hermana Que Fue Maniatada Por el Miedo: Performance Política y Políticas de la Memoria en Antígona, de Yuyachkani." *Hispanic Issues on Line*, vol. 17, no. 17, 2016, pp .126–43.

Roisman, Hanna M. "The Two Sisters." *Looking at Antigone*, edited by David Stuttart, Bloomsbury Academic, 2018, pp. 63–77.

Santiago, Silviano. *The Space In-Between: Essays on Latin American Culture*. Duke University Press. 2001, https://doi-org.ezproxy.cul.columbia.edu/10.1215/9780822383321.

Sedgwick, Eve Kosofsky. *Touching/Feeling: Affect, Pedagogy, Performativity*. Duke University Press, 2003, https://doi-org.ezproxy.cul.columbia.edu/10.1215/9780 822384786.

Sedgwick, Eve Kosofsky and Adam Frank. *Shame and its Sisters: A Silvan Tomkins Reader*. Duke University Press, 1995.

Smethurst, Mae J. "Are we all Creons and Ismenes?" Mee and Foley, pp. 221–34.

Söderbäck, Fanny. *Feminist Readings of Antigone*. E-book, State University of New York Press, 2010.

Steinmeyer, Elke. "Cultural Identities: Appropriations of Greek Tragedy in Post-Colonial Discourse." Liapis and Sidiropoulou, pp. 299–328.

Taylor, Diana. "Staging Traumatic Memory." *The Archive and the Repertoire: Performing Cultural Memory in the Americas*. Duke University Press, 2003, pp. 190–211.

Tiffin, Helen. "Post-Colonial Literatures and Counter-Discourse." *The Post-Colonial Studies Reader*, edited by Bill Ashcroft et al., Routledge, 1995, pp. 95–8.

Weiner, Jesse. "Antigone Undead: Tragedy and Biopolitics in Perla de la Rosa's *Antígona: Las Voces que Incendian el Desierto*." Andújar and Nikoloutsos, pp. 199–212.

Wilmer, Stephen Elliot and Audrone Zukauskaite, editors. *Interrogating Antigone in Postmodern Philosophy and Criticism*. Oxford University Press, 2010, https://oxford- universitypressscholarship com.ezproxy.cul.columbia.edu/ view/10.1093/acprof:oso/9780199559213.001.0001/acpro f-9780199559213.

Worman, Nancy. *Tragic Bodies. Edges of the Human in Greek Drama*. E-book, Bloomsbury, 2020.

———. "Euripides and the Aesthetics of Embodiment." *Brill Companion to Euripides*, edited by Andreas Markantonatos, vol. 1, e-book, Brill, 2020, pp. 749–74.

———. "Touching, Proximity, and the Aesthetics of Pain in Sophocles." Purves, pp. 34–49.

Young, Robert. 2012. "Postcolonial Remains." *New Literary History*, vol. 43, no. 1, pp. 19–42.

APPENDIX

PRODUCTIONS OF JOSÉ WATANABE'S *ANTÍGONA*

Since 2004, at least twelve different theater companies have produced Watanabe's *Antígona* in Argentina, Mexico, Colombia, Venezuela, and Cuba, some of them also touring to other countries in South America, Spain, and the Czech Republic. I have chosen four of these productions, staged after Ralli's original performance in 2000, for a brief discussion of *Antígona*'s afterlife. My main objective is to provide the readers with a diverse sample of directorial choices, which should contribute to a better understanding of the malleability of the text when it comes to the staging. The selected productions also support and expand the readings that I am proposing in this book, at least in two ways: all of them have been produced in countries other than Peru without requiring modifications to the text in order to adapt it to the new contexts, proving the text's capacity to be recontextualized and to remember different events; and, unlike Ralli's original one-woman show, three out of these four productions stage the text with more than one actor, a directorial decision that speaks to the richness of *Antígona*'s formal possibilities and also changes the gender dynamics of the text.

Antígona in Buenos Aires

Directed by Carlos Ianni from the theater organization CELCIT in Buenos Aires, Ana Yovino produced *Antígona* in 2005 (the play has since remained in their repertoire). Yovino and Ianni's version is, like Ralli's, a one-woman show, but where Ralli is intensely physical and employs a series of semiotically charged objects, Yovino is sparing in her gestures and relies almost exclusively on subtle changes in the quality of her voice. This minimalist staging entrusts almost all the work to the poetry of the text as it is heard by the audience.

Antígona in Mexico City

Also from 2005 is Teatro del Mar's production in Mexico City, directed by Miguel Angel Rivera. Four actors (two female and two male) perform all the characters and employ a variety of discards (bandages, plastic fabrics, trash bags, PVC tubes, etc.) to generate a set on the spot evocative of a post-industrial, apocalyptic landscape. The most appealing directorial choice in this staging is that it transforms the predominantly monologic form of the text into a chorus.

Antígona in Cuba

Teatro La Fortaleza's production from 2011 in the town of Cienfuegos, Cuba, is, to my knowledge, the freest adaptation of the text to the stage. The director Atilio Caballero decided to add an extra narrative frame, setting *Antígona* in a new fictional context completely foreign to Watanabe's. The play is performed as a game, played in secret by three museum guards in the context of a Greek art exhibition. Three actresses play the roles of the museum guards and alternate the roles of the characters of *Antígona* as they tell each other the story. This directorial decision fleshes out the meta-theatricality implicit in Watanabe's exercise of re-writing the Greek. The additional narrative frame makes it obvious that these Greek tragedies are stories that we continue to tell ourselves. In this sense, this production adds yet another layer to the complexities of transmission and reception already explored in the text.

Antígona in Venezuela and the Czech Republic

Finally, Carlos Dimeo produced *Antígona* in 2008 in Venezuela and again in 2017–2018 in the Czech Republic. This version showcases ten female actors. The multiplication of the female bodies and voices on stage adds a particularly gendered twist that captures the predominance of the feminine voice in Watanabe's piece. By collectivizing the voice of the narrator Ismene through the use of a female chorus, this production makes more obvious the text's implicit invitation to its audiences to identify with the role of the female witness.

None of these productions modify the text in order to make an obvious connection with the new performative contexts, and, except for La Fortaleza's, all the sets share a sense of topographic abstraction. The set of CELCIT's production has only three ropes hanging from the ceiling of the stage, without making any suggestion of a particular locale but rather proposing an abstract and poetic topography. Teatro del Mar's version locates the action in a post-apocalyptic scenario, yet the place remains rather suggestive and abstract—for one, no modification is made to the text in order to justify the characters' presence in this landscape. Even La Fuerza's production, although in appearance an exception to the rule, nevertheless turns out to prove it: for if it is true that it gives a specific location to the play (a museum), it does so only by adding a foreign narrative frame. Yet, if in this case the space loses its abstract quality, the new frame makes it more explicit that the play is an exercise of memory: the three museum guards remember *Antígona,* or even better, they remember Sophocles' *Antigone* through *Antígona.*

INDEX

Note: Page numbers followed by "n" denote endnotes.

9780367713362